D1596289

Echoes Of A Haunting

A House in the Country

By Clara M. Miller

"Echoes of A Haunting Revisited," by Clara M. Miller. ISBN 978-1-60264-458-8 (softcover) 978-1-60264-459-5 (hardcover).

Published 2009 by Virtualbookworm.com Publishing Inc., P.O. Box 9949, College Station, TX 77842, US. ©2009, Clara M. Miller. All rights reserved. No part of this publication may be reproduced, stored in a retrieval system, or transmitted in any form or by any means, electronic, mechanical, recording or otherwise, without the prior written permission of Clara M. Miller.

Manufactured in the United States of America.

This book is lovingly dedicated to:
My father: Vincent John Miller (1/21/10–6/9/79)
My daughter: Laura Marie Dandy Patron (9/19/60–9/1/92)
My brother: Martin Raymond Miller (7/24/37–1/3/96)
My brother: Gordon Francis Miller (9/17/41–5/17/96)
My uncle: William "Bill" Boland (4/7/02–7/11/84)

Other books by Clara M. Miller

Non-Fiction:
  Echoes of a Haunting (1999)
Fiction:
  The Brothers Series:
    Brothers (2001)
    Once a Demon (2002)
    Birds of a Feather (2002)
    Cirque Diabolique (2003)
    Dancing with Shadows (2007)
    The Uncaused Cause (2007)
    The Brink of Chaos (2007)
  The Shamrocks Saga:
    Shamrocks in the Heather (2003)
    A Breath of Old Smoke (2004)
    Daughters of Gemini (2004)
    Under the Southern Cross (2004)
    Path to Destiny (2005)
    The Eye of the Storm (2005)
    The Sons of the Fathers (2005)
    The Cranky Crow (2008)
    The Devil's Teardrop (2008)
    A Lion in Shadow (2009)
    Odds Bodkins (2009)
  The Saga of the Travelers:
    The Reluctant Heretic (2006)
    Alien Landscape (2006)

Contents

M emories are peculiar things. They come and go, shift and re-shift. They delude and then return with an awful clarity and truth. It's easy to fool yourself. Everyone has a tendency to portray themselves in the best light possible. But, deluding ourselves or not, the core of memory is the truth. Thus it is for me and the house in Hinsdale. Years have passed since I wrote the book about living in the house. More years have passed since I lived there. Still, for almost five hectic years our family stayed in that house, laughed in that house, loved in that house and, ultimately, fled from that house. Do I sound like a coward? Perhaps I am but, as the abyss of time widens between me and the happenings in Hinsdale, I find myself profoundly conflicted. On the one hand, I really miss the place. Not the haunting, certainly, but the life-style we'd established there. In spite of scary interruptions, we enjoyed our rural retreat. I look back on it with great nostalgia and tend to block out the more frightening aspects. Is that denial? I have heard so many people echoing the same sentiment, I know I'm not alone. There's a terrible allure about the place. Those who tend toward addictive personalities should avoid it like the plague.

So many things have happened since we left Hinsdale. Please forgive me if this repeats what I've said at the end when I'm bringing you up to date but a little foreknowledge can be very helpful. Phil and I were divorced in 1980 and he died on August 5, 2002. Mike is living in Oregon and has two sons and daughter. Even more astonishing to me: he has two grandchildren. Beth is living in Virginia with her husband. She has a daughter, a son and two grandsons! Am I getting old? No way. Laura was living in San Jose, California when she died on September 1, 1992. Though she may not know it, she too is a grandma. Mary lives in California. She has two sons. No grandchildren yet. Whew!

I worked for the City of Santa Clara for 15 years before retiring to Oregon. Life is peaceful here on the coast. No ghosts. At least we don't have any ghosts. I'm told the Oregon coast hosts quite a few. I'm not looking for them.

Since I retired, I've passed my time in writing, first my memories of Hinsdale and then fantasy fiction. It's relaxing and I feel at least semi-productive. My mother still lives with me since my father died in 1979. We two old ladies make out just fine, thank you. I confess that mum and I watch all the "ghost-hunting" shows, sometimes with amusement. The cast members startle so easily! I would like to know, though, why they all turn the lights out. Some of our most frightening experiences happened in broad daylight. The only thing I can figure out is that darkness makes it scarier for the viewer at home. It certainly does nothing for the nerves of the "investigators". Mary says that she was sitting in her bed one bright morning having a tug-of-war with something she couldn't see. No darkness then. Ah, well. What do I know?

Now things are heating up again at the house in Hinsdale. I can't say I'm surprised as they've never truly cooled down. The area is saturated with some kind of power I can't define. The times when it's quiescent, you couldn't find a better place to live. Then, it seems to build up and needs a place to vent. If you're there at that point, God help you. The whole nature of the area changes. We called nights like these "umbrella nights". I have yet to find a better description. That's exactly what it felt like. An umbrella descended on the house condensing the power into something very tangible. You didn't have to be psychic to feel it. It affected different people different ways. Some grew increasingly restive. Some became contentious. Some felt their nerves jumping like out-of-control acrobats. There was a sense of expectation, of waiting for the other shoe to drop. See, it's hard to describe. I guess you had to be there.

To anyone who has bought and (I hope) read the previous edition of this book: most of the material herein is unchanged except for corrections in grammar, facts and otherwise. Any additions have been made in italics so you'll know it's new material. That will also help anyone who only wants to skim through and find the new parts. I was very circumspect in the original manuscript because I know too well the price you pay for the doubts of others. But, I've decided to trust you and include some of them in this edition. I will ask you to please put aside your preconceptions and prejudices as you read. We, too, were normal. We, too, were doubters. We, too, led nondescript lives, interchangeable with millions of others. We, too, might have scoffed at the following story. So, this is a kind of cautionary tale. Keep your mind open to things you can't see or hear. Know that we are not omniscient. In my other books I frequently quote Shakespeare since he really got it right: "There are more things in heaven and earth, Horatio, than are dreamt of in your philosophy."

Also, in the interest of full-disclosure, I will tell you that this was not my first encounter with the supernatural. When I was in the last half of eighth grade we moved to a large house quite near my new high school. My father had some friends I didn't know who were helping us move. I discovered clothing in the attic that dated from the early and mid-eighteen hundreds. I hauled them downstairs and sat in the empty closet in my empty bedroom looking them over. My bedroom was directly across from the attic door. Dad told me they were going back for another load and assured me he'd lock the door behind him. I just nodded, caught up in my mental journey to the past. I felt someone watching me but felt no cause for alarm. Finally, when the feeling persisted, I looked up and saw a young man watching me. He stood in the doorway of my bedroom and was dressed in casual gray slacks and a dark blue jacket. He leaned nonchalantly against the door frame. I was a little miffed that my dad didn't trust me alone in the house so I snubbed him and turned back to the clothing. When I looked up again, he was gone. *Serves him right,* I thought.

After a while I heard my father return. When I saw him, I mentioned the man. He said no one had been in the house but me. It kind of jolted me but I shrugged it off. The clothing was stored in the attic. From that day until the day the clothes cabinet was moved, we heard footsteps crossing the attic floor and coming down the stairs. It never frightened anyone and I never found out who the man could have been. Needless to say, this friendly haunt did not prepare me for Hinsdale.

Now, at this late date, I feel constrained to comment on the book I began writing after we'd escaped the house. At first, I couldn't decide how to do this. I hoped to improve on the diary format and discovered that that format suited the tale better than any other. Then I figured the best way was to copy what I'd written before, paraphrasing and commenting as necessary. I have added a few of the more incredible things that happened though the dates of some of these events escapes me. I hope this re-writing doesn't make anyone feel cheated but so many people have told me they can't find copies of my book, maybe they won't mind so much. So, here goes, an experiment in the making.

Echoes of a Haunting

In our innocense we're blind
To things we don't expect to see.
Then opens wide an unknown door,
A door into eternity.

And from that door the echoes flow
Like ripples in a tranquil pond;
Cresting, growing, reaching out,
Engulfing, flooding all beyond.

And still the ripples billow forth
Until they reach the far-flung shore,
But do they stop or merely pause
To echo on forevermore?

The years have passed; the time has flown.
Kith and kin have scattered forth.
Time heals all wounds, the wise men say
But time and tide have finite worth.

For still I feel the echoes peal
And, yes, they touch me even yet.
How can I recall their feel?
But tell me, how can I forget?

To you, my friend, I wish the best
May all your rippling echoes lead
To much more pleasant memories
Than those you are about to read.

cmm

PROLOGUE

I n the first place, the house doesn't even look haunted. If it had soaring battlements, secret passages or ominous looking towers it might be easier to accept what happened there. None of the usual trappings of Gothic novels are present in this normal, rather mundane looking building. How, then, were we to suspect? If we had known its secret, perhaps we never would have bought the house. Perhaps. *That day, the day Donna took us to see the place, we were hooked. Later, that tendency to become drawn to, absorbed in and sometimes obsessed with the house, became more apparent but, on this day, it gave us hope for a brighter future. Little did we know.*

In reality, it was a very ordinary looking farm house, typical for the southern New York State area. Its age, over one hundred years, didn't add distinction. In fact, it didn't even look its age. When we first saw its cheery, newly-painted white exterior, we fell in love. Its luminous appearance made it visible from the main road. The only structure on the side road, it occupied a spot a good half mile from its nearest neighbor. The view of the house disappeared as one turned off the gravel-surfaced main road. After crossing a stream, the narrow dirt road passed a deserted, falling-down shed. From there, it climbed a small hill and turned a bend. At this point the house reappeared.

One half of the house had two stories while the other had only one. *To me, the house was oddly laid out but my husband assured me it was a typical farm house. A front porch was built across the one-story side. Standing on that porch was akin to a spiritual experience. Framed in the windows was a view of hills marching off into the distance. In the autumn those hills were covered with a display of color that would put an ancient tapestry to shame. More than one person gasped at encountering that view. The only house nearby was directly across from us at a distance of about half a mile. Please don't take my measurements of distance literally because I'm measurement-challenged. In effect, we had no near neighbors. Strangely, that didn't bother me.*

Each window *in the house* framed an enchanting view of distant mountains, trees dressed according to the season and ponds, sparkling in the sun. There was nothing sinister appearing about the tall pine tree marking the beginning of the drive. There was nothing spooky about the spring house filled with clear, cold spring water which sparkled to the rear of the yard. There was nothing threatening in the sight of the large pond at the side of the house. *The pond was newly dug and a perimeter of raw earth made the area look injured somehow. But, I assured myself, grass would soon cover the dirt and we'd have a great swimming hole. That pond, it turned out, held many questions, questions that have yet to be answered.* Nor was there anything ominous in the abundance of nature's beauty surrounding the house.

In short, there was nothing in its appearance to warn anyone. How could we have known that it also formed a door to another world? A world I still find difficulty accepting and am unable to describe adequately. A world where values turn upside down and things you have always taken for granted become foreign and threatening. A world which opened up and enmeshed our family in its frightening coils.

The tall, graceful pine standing sentinel at the edge of the curving dirt driveway made an impressive entryway. I loved that pine tree and still remember the sound of the wind soughing through its branches as I lay in bed. It was the only sound one could hear in the early morning hush. No reverberation of traffic penetrated our sanctuary; no noise but those instigated by nature. To our city-bred ears the silence was heavenly.

The back yard was large and had plenty of room for a picnic table and a shed. The remaining area provided more than enough room for all kinds of games. We consumed many carefree meals in that yard and the kids were able to swim in the pond with their friends any time they wanted. *In winter we all donned skates and had fun trying to stay upright.* We had an idyllic existence.....at first.

Looking back, it's hard to figure the whole affair out. How could a family as normal and run of the mill as ours ever come to have such an extraordinary experience? To begin, I guess I'd better tell you a little bit about our family. I was born in 1935 in Buffalo, New York and raised in Irish/German South Buffalo. My husband, Phil, was born in Burdine, Kentucky in 1933 and raised in the rural part of Virginia. He was, therefore, much more familiar with country life than I was. We met in 1954. He was working in the corner grocery store until he found a more suitable job. As I learned later, he had served in the Air Force with the son of the store's owners. After much furtive questioning, I found out he had fled Virginia to avoid a life of toil in the coal mines. His soft, southern accent was very appealing, although, as a staccato-talking Buffalonian, I was impatient with his slow drawl.

Phil and I married in July 1955 and my name changed from Miller to Dandy. Our four children were born in Buffalo and spent their first, formative years there. Mike was born in 1956, Beth in 1957, Laura in 1960 and Mary in 1962. Our fifth baby, Christina Michelle, died in May 1963 when she was only a couple of days old.

I was, at that time, a devout Roman Catholic. I had attended a Catholic grammar school and a Catholic Academy while Phil had no real religion at all. Although he converted to Catholicism before our marriage, I don't think it ever really took. Our relationship suffered from the clash of cultures and backgrounds. I realize now that these differences doomed our marriage from the outset. I was a convent-educated prude while he was a free-wheeling product of an entirely different upbringing. The time he spent in the military did nothing to mellow his personality. Over the years we grew apart, Phil and I. The growing difficulty in our marriage was, perhaps, the reason that I first proposed a vacation. I suggested we spend some time at a cabin near Allegany State Park. A vacation spent together as a family would, I felt, do much to repair the damage.

The year was 1967. Friends of ours owned a cabin right outside the park and we decided to rent it for a week in the summer. For those not familiar with it, Allegany State Park is very rugged and filled with deep forests and trails. An extremely beautiful, back-to-nature place, I felt that its peace would have a beneficial effect on all of us. The cabin itself sat on an isolated lot near the park. Its construction was rather primitive, made with salvaged materials. Its hodge-podge origin showed. There was a separate, spare sleeping shed build like a detached porch about twenty feet from the main house.

Each morning we woke to heavy mountain fog that burned off before noon. Our family spent blissful days tramping around the woods or driving through the park itself to look for wild animals. Mike spent a lot of his time hunting snakes and efts. In fact, he took home several red-bellied racers and regular garden snakes which gave us some interesting exercise when they got loose in the house. The kids thrived in the relaxed atmosphere and we went home with reluctance.

So it was, that in the autumn following our cabin vacation, we began looking for our own cabin to buy. We had loved the area so we concentrated on property near the park. After much scrutiny, that winter we saw an ad for cabins in the Buffalo newspaper. It sounded ideal, since they were only about a half hour's drive from Allegany Park. With a sense of triumph, we determined to investigate.

The following Sunday found us driving the winter-slick roads to look at what the sellers had to offer. The people who placed the ad, Ken and Donna R, ran a game farm in the area. As a side-line, they built small cabins to sell to people like us who were weary of city life. One of the cabins shown us was *in West Clarksville*, near Cuba, New York and sat about half way up a steep hill. When we first saw it, the owners hadn't quite completed construction of the tiny building but we fell in love with it anyway. By the end of the week, we were the proud owners of the cabin and three acres of land. The cabin had a redwood exterior with a general overhang sheltering a terrace of fieldstone. Inside was a large combination living room/kitchen, two bedrooms and a full bath. The picture window in the front looked out over the patio to a stand of pine and maple trees. From one side of the building was a view of a tree-filled gully. The back window showed our as yet unfinished hilly yard. The view from the other side showed the steep driveway leading through a tunnel of trees to the road.

At that time, I was working as an office manager at the State University College of New York at Buffalo. Phil had a good job as a crane operator for the Ford Motor company. The two salaries meant we could easily afford the payments on the now unbelievable sounding price of $5,800. Even with paying for the addition of a well installed shortly after buying the place, it was a bargain.

Every weekend when the weather turned pleasant, we would escape from the rush of the city and find peace in our quiet retreat. When I look back on the carefree, happy times we spent in that cabin, I really regret ever letting it go. As time went on, however, my well-meant plans began to go awry. Phil no longer accompanied us. My girlfriend, Shirl, the kids and I were the usual weekend occupants.

Still, I loved the place. I continued to hold hopes that Phil would one day see it with the same eyes we did. Looking back, I wonder if he didn't relish the times when we were at the cabin and he became a temporary bachelor again. Perhaps that's unkind of me but the thought persists. Gradually, we met other cabin owners in the area and became friends with the family living in a "real house" next door. Their son and daughter became friends.

Campers down the road, Buffalonians also, traded visits with us. A family of four, they always welcomed us although their site had no cabin but only a small camper. Their daughter, Nancy, became a close friend to Beth. Gary, their older son had recently returned from Vietnam and was attending the same College where I worked. In short, we felt right at home.

Every weekend we explored the woods and the surrounding towns, sometimes with the kids' newly-made friends in tow. We found the town of Obi where the white deer came down to feed at twilight, looking for all the world like graceful ghosts. We bought cheese from the Cuba Cheese Factory. We drove all the way to Corning to tour the Glass Factory. On hot summer days, we waded down a nearby stream looking for crawdads and planaria. To the consternation of the guardian jays, we walked the nearby woods, our wondering, neophyte eyes taking in everything at once. I finally learned not to wear my ersatz fur cap. To my complete astonishment, my family told me it made me look like a deer's rear end to a hunter. Hunting season was always an anxious time for us. Not only did we dread seeing the deer carcasses slung proudly on gory fenders but we feared we might accidentally become targets for some overenthusiastic "sportsman".

In "our" woods we found a tree obviously occupied by possums. The little family lived in the tree and used its hollow interior as an outhouse. Instead of a septic tank, it emptied though a wide gash at the bottom of the tree resulting in a rather odorous pile about four feet high. Laughingly, we called it the "mystery tree". One trip up a nearby mountain resulted in panic. As we climbed, we heard a loud, deep growl. The dogs went to investigate: our spaniel, Binky, and our neighbors' two dogs. Mary made a beeline for our cabin, sure it was a bear, but I couldn't leave the dogs to face a possible bear. Upon investigation, we found the growler was a large porcupine. Another lesson learned–I hadn't known that porcupines growled. Cautious Binky got only one quill in his nose before calling it quits but the other two dogs got a real snootful. We had to take them to the vet. We returned to the cabin and found my mother and father trying to console Mary. She was sure she was an orphan. Before she would open the door for them, they had to identify themselves as human, not bears. Ever practical, Mary had asked my mother if she'd cook for her if a bear had eaten me.

All in all, it was a wonderful time for us. I hope the kids have as enjoyable memories of that period as I do. At any rate, the cabin gave us our first real taste of country life and we liked it.

In retrospect, it seems as though we were on a preordained course and perhaps the house was an unchangeable part of our future. Perhaps it was waiting for us. I could go on and on with philosophical musings about the whys and wherefores and all the *if's, ands* or *buts* but it would do little to alter the facts. We were on a collision course with destiny.

Whatever conjectures I come up with, the fact remains, there came a time when just a weekend retreat was not enough. Each time we returned home, the crowds, noise and dirt seemed more apparent. The few times Phil had visited the cabin had given him the same craving for a quieter life. Or so I thought, anyway. *Ever the optimist!*

I know in the present day and age we are not unique in wanting to escape the confines of the city. Still, it involved much soul-searching since it would be such a drastic change for all of us. For one thing, I wasn't at all sure I could take the long commute to Buffalo every day–about 75 miles each way. Phil could stay with my mother and father in Buffalo if it got too rough but I couldn't leave the kids alone. The move might entail quitting my job, a job I loved and couldn't afford to lose.

Then too, we had to consider that the kids would be leaving all their friends. Although I was sure they could make new ones, it is a difficult thing for a child to face. In addition, they would have to transfer from a sheltered Catholic school to a public school. That alone might be a difficult adjustment for them. We talked it over, all of us, and finally decided to give it a try.

First, we thought of building a house on the cabin property, a place we already loved. But the woman who sold us the cabin told us she had a farm house for sale in the same general area. She was most convincing when she told us it was just right for our family. We agreed to wait until the repairs on the century-old house were complete and we would decide after seeing the property. There followed a period of unbearable waiting. Since we had made up our minds, we were anxious to put our plans into motion.

The day finally arrived when we were to see the house. The four kids were running around, getting ready, in an almost holiday spirit. It was useless to try to quiet them and, since Phil and I felt the same excitement, we had no real inclination to do so. We were going to see our house! Already we felt it was our house, though we had yet to see it. All portents were good. It was a clear spring day and, though chilly, was very pleasant. With much scurrying and going back for Mary's teddy bear ("Bunny wants to go too!") and, of course, last minute bathroom stops, we finally got on the road. The distance was not so great—about 65 or 70 miles and it took us through some spectacular scenery. The earth was waking up with fresh greenery everywhere. Rivulets of water ran down hills at the edge of the road and deer were coming down to sample the tender young shoots. The deer provided a much needed distraction for the still overexcited kids and they managed to count 74 of them during the trip. As usual, I worried about having the proper papers; finding the place and liking it. Phil assured me everything would be all right. Following directions, we climbed Wagner Hill Road and then descended the other side part way to the turn at McMahon Road. The narrow dirt road passed a stream and an old barn; then took a sharp turn left. There it was—our house! It looked so welcoming—as though it had been expecting us. And we felt as though we were home. The car couldn't make it any further through the deep mud so we slogged the rest of the way and awaited the arrival of the present owner. She soon arrived in a four wheel drive vehicle and showed us around. She knew she had us sold when the kids began to claim bedrooms.

There was never any doubt in our minds, we knew it was for us. Situated about four miles from the town of Hinsdale, it sat rather importantly in its own little protected pocket of land. Surrounded by heavily wooded hills, it sported a newly-dug pond sitting to one side. How the kids loved that pond! All in all, the property consisted of eight acres. The single story half of the house contained a country-style kitchen, a utility room and a bedroom. The lower story of the other side boasted the living room, a bedroom and the bath. *There was a door in the kitchen and one in the living room both of which exited onto the porch. Since we really needed a coat closet and didn't need another exit, dad and Phil built a closet out of the entrance from the living room. It proved a God-send.* The upstairs had one good sized bedroom, a small bedroom and a closet masquerading as another bedroom.

Facing the dangerously steep stairs as one descended was the door to a crawl space—a feature of the house with which I was not familiar. Having always lived in houses with attics, the awkward crawl space was not my idea of a storage space. It was peak-roofed and almost inaccessible. *The only way to enter was by balancing a plank on the narrow sides of the stairway or on the stairs themselves and tightrope walking across.* When the door was open, hot, dusty air rushed out. Looking in, one could see the neat, brick chimney among the angled rafters.

Another feature of the house which offended my city sensibilities was a root cellar. Now, I have lived in houses containing cellars all my life. I have always found them to be efficient storage spaces, convenient laundry rooms and very good locations for children's parties. But the root cellar was something else again. The only entrance was through a rather narrow door set in the bathroom, of all places, about a foot from the toilet. One would find it difficult to imagine a more awkward location. If the cellar itself hadn't been so dreary, perhaps the oddly-placed door wouldn't have been so bad. But descending the rickety stairs and coming to the dirt floor made my flesh crawl. The side walls were rough-hewn stone. *To the left of the stairs as you descend you could actually look under the foundation. A good place for animals to hide.* There was only a small area in which the ceiling was high enough to allow one to stand. The "dungeon" had no virtues that I could see. In fact, after taking one look at it, I uttered the portentous words "Vincent Price lives down there!" Later we came to recall those words with more than a slight shudder. My profound apologies to Vincent Price!

In spite of its many faults, we fell under the enchantment of the place. The panoramic scenes visible from every window were truly breathtaking. The thought of owning such a place and getting a pond and eight acres besides was intoxicating. It didn't take us long to trade our cabin in for the house. Thus it began.

As the spring weather improved, we, that is the kids and I, began to take trips to the house. Doggedly, we started moving some of the smaller items in our station wagon. Since to reach our house we had to drive two and one half miles of dirt road, the spring rains presented a definite moving problem. On one of our mini-moving trips the first of our soon-to-be-famous car trouble occurred. My mother and I took the kids down so the telephone company could install our telephone. I may like to rough it but I like to do it in comfort–and safety! As far as I was concerned, a telephone was a necessity living so far from town.

Our car, which up to now had given us no trouble, suddenly overheated and boiled over. Luckily, the man from the telephone company helped us and we were able to make it back to Buffalo. The station wagon was a 1970 model and, from that day on, radiator problems plagued us until we got rid of the car. There was no way I could have known it then but this signaled the beginning of constant car trouble. Trouble that struck not only us but many people who visited us.

In the fall, one of my co-workers had offered to give us a kitten for Laura's birthday. Ethel M insisted that country living required a mouser. I agreed and Laura became the proud owner of a most remarkable cat, aptly named Fluffy. She was to become a tiny, indefatigable protector against the worst the house could offer. During one of our trips to the house, though, she gave us a quite a start. She disappeared. For about an hour we looked high and low for her. Laura cried and swore that she wouldn't leave without her. Finally, we found her curled up in an opening made for an electrical outlet. Yes, she was that tiny. Ethel hadn't been just bragging about Fluffy's abilities. Not only did she teach all of our succeeding cats to hunt mice and other rodents but she litter-trained all of them too. In fact, she litter-trained our raccoon, Princess. The only problem was that Princess had hands and couldn't properly neaten the litter after she used it. This lack brought reproving looks from Fluffy, whereupon, she'd take it upon herself to do the housekeeping duties.

One day I saw her sitting at the side of the spring house seemingly waving her paws in the air. Puzzled, I walked across the yard to investigate. She had found a nest of water snakes and was busily and calmly cutting them to bits with her claws. I watched, fascinated, as she actually sliced them up. We never had snakes in that area again.

Chapter 1

A House in the Country

THE MOVE-July 18, 1970

After what seemed an eternity, moving day finally arrived. My mother and younger brother, Gordon, went ahead with our clothes in his car. I wasn't to find out what greeted them until hours later. When they arrived they found the house completely filled with bees. Every window was so black with them it was impossible to see out. During all our mini-moves we hadn't seen one bee. How they could have accumulated so quickly still baffles me. Consultation later with a bee expert told us that it was unnatural for them to swarm at that time of the year. Gordon had to brave the almost solid phalanx of swarming, buzzing insects to reach the phone and call an exterminator. The exterminator, astounded by both the number of bees and their strange behavior, sprayed the house and assured them the spray was safe for humans and animals. Thus it was that, before we even moved in, we had to pay $75 to rid the house of our unwanted guests. Our arrival, then, soon after was greeted by piles of dead bees–bodies everywhere. Mum and Gordon had been busy since the exterminator left sweeping them up. There were grocery bags full of them and still they covered the floor. We were troubled for many months by minor incidents with bees, including honey dripping off our ceiling until finally the queen bee had had enough and drew the swarm to better and, I presume, more welcoming, quarters.

Dad was driving a big moving truck with the bulk of our furniture and Phil a borrowed pickup truck carrying the rest. On the way, however, my father took a wrong turn and got lost. Laura was with him and we had some very anxious moments until they finally pulled in the driveway. I formed the caboose of our caravan and brought my oldest daughter, Beth, my youngest daughter, Mary and all the pets.

At that time the pet contingent consisted of two dogs (Binky and Tyger), a cat (Fluffy), a raccoon (Princess), four guinea pigs, two parakeets, two finches and a woodchuck (Nipper). Naturally, our old reliable station wagon boiled over before it had gone 20 miles. The outside temperature was over eighty degrees so I had some coolant put in the radiator and prayed the rest of the way. It was now July 18, 1970.

When we arrived, the smell of the chemical the exterminator had used still filled the house. The man assured us it was harmless to humans and animals, so the kids and I decided to stay. I felt a deep sense of relief when Gordon offered to stay with us. Phil had to return the borrowed truck and would drive his own car back in the morning. Dad and mum returned home in the truck.

Now, we got a closer look at the house. At first glance it had the drawbacks I have already mentioned. The dank, dark root cellar always topped my list. Whoever designed the dark crawl space, almost inaccessible, above the kitchen did not intend it for storage. The heating system was archaic and inadequate and the gravity-fed spring water was unreliable at best. *The "furnace" was in a hole in the living room floor. You had to drop a match in to light it! Are you surprised we replaced it? I didn't find out until sometime later that our septic tank was an old oil drum! I knew nothing about septic tanks at that point anyway.* Everyone assured me that my apprehensions came from my big city upbringing. Phil assured me that all root cellars were the same. Gradually, he told me, we could correct most of the faults. Looking back, I wish these physical shortcomings had been the only problems we had to face.

After talking it over, we decided to let our woodchuck, Nipper, go free when we arrived as we thought she'd be happier in the woods. With many tears, Beth opened the cage, whereupon Nipper promptly darted out and right into the house. For three days we couldn't find her amid the piled-up furniture and boxes. We knew she was still around as our supply of apples was mysteriously disappearing. Once we had the furniture arranged, however, Nipper decided she'd like it better outside after all.

Up until the supper of 1972, Nipper paid regular visits to the house for handouts. Hearing noises at the crawl space door, we'd open it to find a hungry looking woodchuck asking for her favorite food, oatmeal cookies. Unfortunately, this special treat was not available in the woods. I know her home was washed out during the flood in the spring of 1972. She took refuge with us and was a very wet and bedraggled looking animal. By her condition, she had obviously just had babies and, by her distress and the way she clung to my hand, it was painfully clear that she must have lost them as well as her home. In her sorrow, she allowed me to cuddle her and hold her on my lap like a baby. Hopefully, I was some consolation to her. After sheltering with us until she the worst was over and the water level dropped, she left and must have moved some distance away as we never saw her again. I prefer that explanation to the more difficult one of a hunter or farmer shooting her as a "pest". *Another victim of the flood was our much-loved raccoon, Princess. She had been caught in a trap once before. The trap was set in a nearby ravine. A couple of hunters saw her and were surprised that she seemed to be asking for help. They freed her and she raced home. She must have gotten caught in another trap just before the flood hit. I still have nightmares about that.*

During this settling-in period, the dogs began bringing home huge, old bones. Each one was unceremoniously disposed of in the garbage. Mistake! However, at the time we didn't know that. *When I think of those bones today, I'm amazed at my casual ignorance. Not knowing what deer bones looked like, I assumed the long bones were animal bones (deer probably). Hindsight: I should have had them checked.*

Once we were settled, I thought I would try going back to work even though it meant driving 150 miles a day. I didn't mind the distance since I love to drive but I had to leave the house shortly after 5 a.m. and didn't get home until 6 p.m., making it a long day and difficult for all of us. However, I learned to use that driving time for a transition from one world to the other. And they did, indeed, seem like different worlds.

My first day back to work was difficult even though my fellow workers had welcome-back signs taped all over the office. It would take a while to get used to the schedule.

That first evening, I came home to the delicious aroma of beef stew Beth had prepared and it lifted my spirits considerably. Maybe this wouldn't be so bad after all. That thought ringing in my mind, I called Mary for supper. She came down the road crying, with blood running down her face. Her bike had hit a rock and she had landed on her chin. Three hours and six stitches later the stew was no longer enticing and I began to wonder about the decision to continue working. Secretly, I also began to question our wisdom in moving.

I managed to hang on at the College until November when I resigned, hoping to transfer to a State job closer to home. In the end, it wasn't so much the distance, the commuting time, or the inconvenience but simply because my work load had increased dramatically with no corresponding increase in help or updated equipment.

I make no claims to being the housewifely type but I found staying home very appealing. For the first time in years I was able to sew clothes for the family, bake and do the things that I used to take for granted before I started working. Knowing the euphoric feeling wouldn't last, I enjoyed it while I could and before the chores became boring.

Shortly after we moved in, the neighbors from across the way came over and introduced themselves. Pat, Bob and Matt's ages roughly coincided with those of our kids so it worked out well. Pat was a pretty brown-haired, freckle-faced pixie. Bob was darker than his sister and was almost as kinetic as Mike. Matt's small elfin face was dwarfed by a large pair of glasses. Their mother, Mary D was younger than I and very pretty. Mary and her daughter, Pat, could have been sisters. Although we didn't get together on a regular basis, she and I visited often and got along famously. The family lived in a ranch style home on a hill across the main road. Since it was at approximately the same level, it was easily visible from our house.

One weekend, while I was still working, I heard some shots nearby. Since the sound of gunfire isn't all that rare in the country. I paid it no attention. Suddenly, the phone rang. Mike and Beth had been with their friends in the field in front of their house when someone began shooting at them. Hugging the ground, they managed to make it to the ranch house. I ran to the car and raced to get over there and pick them up. Only later did it occur to me that whoever was shooting at them might have tried to shoot at me. Answering our anxious questions, the only thing they could remember was that just a few minutes before the shooting started, they had seen the car of a man who lived about two miles away from us. The neighbor in question had a reputation as an eccentric. In fact, he had chased some of our neighbors who had accidentally gotten too close to his house. The conclusion was that it was probably him. At the time, I did nothing about it but took the kids home immediately.

The next morning, I told my boss about the incident and he was appalled. He told me to use the WATS line and call the State Police in our area. The trooper who answered said "Maybe he thought they were woodchucks." My answer, "I don't know about your children, but mine don't look like woodchucks." Nothing, however, was ever done about it.

Not long after meeting us, our young friends told us there was a "ghost" who walked down our road. We laughed and Mike laughed the loudest. However, one day he casually mentioned that he had seen the ghost. Bob and Matt had been walking home with him when they suddenly saw what they took to be a farmer walking ahead of them. The other two boys said it was the ghost so, naturally, Mike decided to chase him. The three boys ran after the apparition along the road and were no more than six feet away from him when he stepped behind an old apple tree at the top of the hill. In spite of the fact that the boys were right behind him, when they reached the tree he had disappeared. There are open fields on all sides of the tree. I don't know why but at the time I didn't take this incident too seriously. In fact, I dismissed it from my mind with a secret sense of tolerant amusement.

As the days went by, I realized that Pat took our ghostly friend quite seriously. While everyone else saw this man as a farmer she insisted he was a "black man", not a Negro, but a "black man". She was absolutely terrified of him. I pored through occult books trying to find a mention of such a specter and was rather sorry when I did. The significance of a "black man" in all the reference books was to Satan. Although I myself don't believe in such a person, it did alarm me concerning Pat's mind-set. One day, I remember, Beth and Pat came running in the house on the verge of hysterics. When they had calmed down a little they told me the "man" had been watching them from the hill. Again, they had each seen him differently. Beth did not agree that the man was "black". Try as I might, I never did get to see our first resident "spook" and, in fact, was not terribly concerned by his presence. Why? I'll never know.

Not too long after we moved in, Mary's dog, Tyger, disappeared. At the time, there were a lot of articles in the paper regarding dogs being shot. For some reason which I cannot hope to fathom, people were using them for target practice. Our dogs usually stayed pretty close to home but we never did find Tyger. A gentle, friendly golden collie, I couldn't imagine anyone wanting to hurt him. Mary was devastated by his disappearance. After waiting for a while to see if he'd return, we took her to the local SPCA to pick out a new dog. In one of the cages was a dog I thought at first was Tyger but, no, this one was a female and she had just had puppies. Since the discovery of Tyger's twin seemed providential, we immediately adopted "Lassie". Had it been up to us, we would have come up with a more original name but she was used to it. Lassie wound up being one the best and nicest dogs we've ever owned.

All my life, I had wanted a St. Bernard. Don't ask me why, I just love them. So, Phil decided I should have one on our second Christmas at the house. He said a friend of his owned a German Shepherd that was due to have puppies and the father was a St. Bernard. That was how we acquired Peanuts. A big, loveable, clumsy dog with a heart as big as the world, he looked like neither his mother nor his father. The first winter we had him, he got in the habit of "skating" on the frozen pond. You haven't lived until you've seen a clumsy puppy skating. When spring thaw came, however, Peanuts galloped out ready to do his regular four legged ballet. Instead, he plunged into icy water. I wish I had a picture of his face. If a dog can be astonished and embarrassed at the same time, Peanuts was.

Our menagerie grew when we acquired a de-scented skunk from our vet. Dolly did not have a stripe down her back but instead, had a white, winged "mustache" on her head and a white tipped tail. Someone had the temerity to suggest that she'd be worth a lot for her fur. The look he got would have frozen boiling water. Then we got a calico cat named "Tish". Actually what Phil called her was something a bit different. I just turned the word sort of backwards and called her Tish. Unfortunately, without my knowing it, she crawled into the dryer and was killed. We replaced her with another Tish but it wasn't the same. I cried for days after her death, blaming myself. I just never thought to check the inside of the machine before turning it on. But now, I see in re-reading this that I've gotten badly off track and I must go back a bit to the beginning.

Chapter 2

T he winter of 1970 proved to be our baptism of fire. It was an unusual winter in two ways. For one thing, it was one of the coldest on record. The temperature dropped to 20 degrees below zero without figuring in the wind factor. In fact, I still have the thermometer to prove it. The poor thing never recovered from the shock and still registers minus 20 degrees. Secondly, the snow almost buried us. On February 1, 1971, our water lines froze and didn't thaw again until late in April. That's when we discovered the treasure we had in the spring house.

We all found muscles we didn't know we had as we strained to haul pails of water through the yard. First, we had to break through the thick ice coating on the surface. This was done with a little hammer, which the kids promptly nicknamed "Mom's Silver Hammer", referring to the Beatle's song. We were each allowed one bath a week because the whole family had to haul water to get enough for the tub. The water had to be heated on the stove and then mixed with cold water (also from the spring house) in the bathtub. A long, tedious process, believe me. The toilet was flushed with pails of water also drawn from our miraculous spring house.

I remember one night it was my turn, at last, to take a bath. Hooray–I couldn't wait! Laboriously, we hauled the water and I waited impatiently while it heated on the stove. Finally, my bath was ready and I went to my room to fetch my pajamas. I returned to find Princess, our raccoon, happily splashing away in **my** water! Looking for all the world like any other bather, she sat up straight and splashed water over her back with her hands. I tried to be furious but it was no use. She looked too funny. Everyone had to come and take a look at her. Pleased as punch that she was amusing us, she managed to put on quite a show. I had to wait a week for my next bath.

In addition to the inconvenient water supply, the wind howled through the house, buffeting drapes, finding its way through unseen openings and chilling us right to the bone. At one point the winds reached gusts of 70 miles an hour, dropping the temperature in the house to an uncomfortable 43 degrees and pointing out the inadequacy of our antiquated heating system. The wind continued for two teeth-chattering days. We were forced to take refuge under electric blankets.

As long as I live, I'll remember hauling water for baths through winds so strong that a full pail of water swung to a position horizontal with the ground. The snow, in the meantime, was so deep on the road that the snowplow got stuck and they had to move the snow out with a high lift. There was beauty, though, in spite of our discomfort. When the wind finally stopped, the snow stood in free-form sculptures all around the yard. The gale had laid the ground bare in some spots and piled the snow up in others. Our prosaic back yard resembled a modern art gallery.

On another occasion, I received a shock I hadn't expected. One evening, while carrying in yet another pail of water, I saw an object in the sky approaching me from the south at a high rate of speed and in complete silence. Quickly, I called to the kids. All five of us watched as the craft, or whatever it was, hovered for a few minutes overhead. Having always laughed derisively at reports of "flying saucers", it was hard to admit what I was seeing. The object, for I refused to call it a UFO, was large and round and appeared to have lighted windows outlining it. As we watched, it veered suddenly and disappeared into the night sky to the north. Do I have an explanation? No, I still don't know what it was. The kids reported seeing similar objects many times in our night sky. Sometimes, they appeared to be executing intricate maneuvers. Writing this is difficult because, judging from my own reaction to such reports, no one is likely to believe me.

One night, the summer following our first winter, we had another scare. Since our house was far from the nearest dwelling, I had gotten in the habit of sleeping with the window shades open. That way, I could look out at the stars whenever I had a sleepless night. This particular night, however, I woke up from a sound sleep to discover the room bathed in a fluorescent light that was so bright it lit up my whole room in sharp relief. The source of the light was definitely over the house. Unwillingly, my mind went to the round object we had seen in the night sky.

Suddenly, I heard Michael's quavery voice calling me from downstairs. "Mom," he said, "do you see it? The whole house is lit up! I think it's right outside my window." His voice was panicky and I struggled to keep calm. Was he right? Was it right outside his window? My common sense told me no, that the light was distributed throughout the house so it must be over us.

As firmly as possible I told him, "I think it's above us, Mike. Just ignore it. Stay in bed and don't go to the window!" I'm not sure what I thought would happen if he were seen but I surely didn't want to find out. As usual, Phil was in Buffalo and we were all alone. For about ten heart-stopping minutes, that light hovered over us. Then abruptly, it was gone.

Through my front window, I could see the same, or a similar, round object heading away from our house at a high speed in an easterly direction. With wonder, I saw it fly over our neighbors' house and disappear in the distant mountains. A few days later, I read in the paper that there were reports of a flying saucer throughout our area. I've been trying to remember locales and dates but, at this remove, cannot do so. I know there were reports from Corning, to the east of us and Little Valley to the northwest. Again, I can offer no explanation, only the story.

Getting back to the subject: Did all the bad weather and strange phenomena discourage us? Not in the least! However, we now knew we had to replace both the heating and water supply systems and put in some kind of insulation. In addition, the wind had shown us the faults of our old windows and we made plans to buy good aluminum storms and screens. This, of course, cost us a great deal of money. Since I was no longer working, the burden fell squarely on Phil.

The heating system, the well, the windows and blown-in insulation set us back about $3,000. We then had a reliable and delicious water supply and could be fairly sure of comfort in both hot and cold weather. The root cellar I would just have to learn to live with. Even with the addition of the new oil furnace, it still looked ominous to me.

I have to tell you about our well. After our lines thawed that first winter, we noticed a horrible taste in the water, water that was provided by a gravity-fed system similar to the one we replaced at the cabin. Upon investigation, we discovered a chipmunk who had the misfortune to drown in our well. We promptly contacted the well-driller who had replaced the system at the cabin. Mr. O lived in Pennsylvania, not too far across the border. When I told him about the chipmunk, he was horrified. With an urgent warning not to drink the water, he promised to come as soon as possible. No such warning was needed but his concern made us feel good.

When he had replaced the well at the cabin, I hadn't had much contact with him so was unprepared for his manner. At first I thought he was kidding me with his "ayup!" answers. But no, he was a true American Gothic and I liked him immediately. His slow, pleasant drawl was soothing somehow and gave the impression that he was extremely dependable. This proved to be true. It was an education for all of us pragmatic city slickers to watch Mr. O dowsing. Carefully, he cut a forked branch and walked over the property. There was no denying it when the branch dipped. Still, he walked around, saying the pull wasn't strong enough. Suddenly, it almost tore itself right out of his hands. This finally satisfied him. With a grin, he told me he had found the confluence of two underground streams. Sure that this conjunction would provide us with more than sufficient water, this is where he dug our well.

Seeing that I was fascinated by his dowsing, he promptly showed me that it worked just as well with a pair of pliers. I almost caught flies in my mouth suddenly agape with astonishment. Another bit of education you don't pick up in schools! The digging itself took some time. Each day he'd come and unload his ancient truck, hook up the drill and begin. The solid thump, thump of the drill soon became a familiar and almost comforting sound. Each night, he'd take the drill apart and haul the bits home to sharpen them. When I enquired, he told me that, unlike some of his counterparts, he believed in keeping his equipment in perfect repair. His answer did not surprise me in the least but was typical of the way he did everything. Then one day, it was done. The pump was lowered into the hole; Mr. O replaced our outdoor faucets with the self-emptying type that wouldn't freeze and he was gone.

The well was deep and our underground pump proved dependable. The water was the most delicious I have ever tasted even to this day. To my surprise, when Mr. O left, we missed him and the continual, solid thump of his drill. The odd silence left a hole in our lives. But, we did have water. Mr. O and his rhythmic, magical drill, however, was one of the few good experiences we were having.

Chapter 3

THE TROUBLE CONTINUES

S ince our initial experience with the bees we had been dogged by bad luck. Strange accidents began plaguing us. Mary's fall from her bike seemed to signal a trend. Not too long afterward, Laura fell from her mini-bike and wound up with a severe staph infection in her foot. Mike spilled boiling water on himself and scalded his stomach. I broke my finger while changing a window and sported a splint for months. Furthermore, it was my right hand so I couldn't even sign my name. Mike cut a tendon in his hand while cutting a glass bottle in preparation for making a vase. Phil cut his thumb to the bone while pushing a car stuck in the snow. Beth feel in gym, breaking her arm. This led to a permanently disfigured arm. Mike broke his toe playing basketball and Laura broke her foot while exercising. My mother, immediately after returning from our house, fell down the stairs and broke her leg.

In addition, my mother and father had three auto accidents while returning from visits. I had an auto accident while Christmas shopping in Buffalo in November of 1971. Mike had a severe auto accident on October 21, 1973 and almost died. Five weeks later, Beth's boyfriend, having just brought his new car up to show us, had an accident and, two years later, was still unable to work.

The list goes on: we had four auto accidents in two weeks in early 1974–Keith, a friend who was staying with us at the time, was going to a school dance in Phil's car. On his way over a narrow bridge, a car with no headlights ran right into him. The boys in Mike's class got together and repaired the damage. A few days later Mike was taking it down the hill in icy weather when the steering wheel refused to respond and he hit a tree. At this point the car had to be replaced. Phil bought a used car from a neighbor. Again, the boys borrowed it to go into Olean and a man ran a red light and plowed right into the side of them. Of course, none of these accidents was covered by insurance. Luckily, Mike's serious accident **was** covered. He used his insurance money to buy a beautiful red 1970 Maverick. Since he planned on going to college, we knew he'd need a reliable car. A week later Phil had to borrow it to go to work. His car was not running the way it should and, besides, he wanted to try the Maverick out on a long trip. As he was on his way home in the middle of the night, a truck approached in his lane and ran him off the road. The car skidded across the road and rolled over three times, pinning him in the car upside down. The police gave him a ticket for failure to keep right.

Besides the accidents, the car trouble we were having was becoming legendary. We had traded our 1970 wagon in on a 1972. Everything that could possibly go wrong with a car went wrong with that one. It got so the service manager in the Agency knew my voice on the telephone. In fact, we were so well known that a relative of one of the Agency employees was able to trace us through the mention of the car trouble in the paper. The problem wasn't just with our cars either. People would drive up to visit and, on parking in our yard, their exhaust systems would fall off or their brakes would fail or their transmissions suddenly refuse to work.

Also alarming to us was the sudden mortality among our animals. We have always had pets and had none die except of old age. However, since we moved into the house we lost: two finches, one canary, one cat, two parakeets, one dog, three guinea pigs and a raccoon. In Mary's room three of the animals, a guinea pig, a canary and a parakeet died within a two month period with no apparent cause. Our vet finally advised us to keep pets out of that room.

In fact, it wasn't too long until we had to keep people out of that room. Suddenly, sums of money began disappearing. Usually small, it nevertheless taxed our limited finances. The money always disappeared when there was no one around to take it and often from a locked container. Our financial situation steadily worsened and we began to have the distinct feeling we weren't wanted in the house. Please remember that all the events described happened within the period we were living in the house, from July 1970 until October 1974. However, we were not alarmed, as yet, by the possibility of spirits.

Does it seem as if we were slow to react? I guess it would to someone who hadn't been there. But, you know, when you're in the middle of strange happenings, it's easier to explain them away or deny they happened than to be forced to re-examine all your preconceived notions. There are no such things as ghosts! There is no such thing as an "unfriendly house"! In addition, these events occurred over a period of time, not all at once. There were "reasonable" explanations for all of them. That is, until you put them all together and the total was more than equal to the sum of individual occurrences.

Trying to find the incidents which puzzled us at the time but now seem to make a macabre kind of sense is a very difficult task. I remember one incident in 1970. I was working at the time and arrived home to find the kids quite upset. They were very uncomfortable and insisted that someone had broken into the house. Since, by this time, we had three big dogs, I found this hard to believe. However, I was forced to admit that someone (using hindsight–something?) had been in the house. The clothes had been pulled out of the drawers in my dresser and the girls' dressers. Neither Phil's nor Mike's clothes had been touched. Money and guns in Mike's room were also still in their usual places in plain sight. Mary's record player had been hurled across her room and lay on the floor in the corner. Our oldest dog, Binky, had been with us for 13 years and could be quite vicious when it came to intruders but, when the kids arrived home, he was slinking around the house. Obviously, he had been frightened by something. Draw your own conclusions. I still have none.

Another threatening incident occurred in the winter of 1972. It was early in the year. Mike and Beth were attending a record hop at school one dreary Friday night. Mike was not yet old enough to drive so I always picked them up at midnight when the dances were over. It was an open winter and I remember there wasn't much snow on the ground. The unsettling thing was that sheets of lightning kept flashing across the sky, lighting the landscape and turning it into an otherworldly tableau. My only companion on the eight mile round trip was Mary's dog, Lassie. Her company kept me from getting too alarmed by the anger of the elements.

We reached the bend in the road just before it begins to dip to a low point. There, it crosses a small stream in a gully and then climbs again to meet the main road. A flash of light suddenly lit up the sky in front of us. Just before the dip in the road is a dead tree next to an old broken down barn or shed. The fallen branches of the tree frequently blocked our way after a wind storm. This night, however, it was not fallen branches that frightened me but the silhouette of a body hanging from the dead tree and swinging in the wind. I saw it long enough to notice that it had a hood or hat over its head but not long enough to know for sure whether it was a man or a woman.

I slammed on the brakes so hard that poor Lassie wound up on the floor. Even though the next lightning flash showed the figure to be gone, no one will ever know how hard it was to drive under that tree. My scalp was prickling and icy fingers were playing havoc with my spine. It's funny how easy it was to dismiss this event from my mind just as we continually dismissed any event we couldn't explain. We just couldn't admit there was something very weird going on. It was much easier to blame it on being unused to country life or being tired or nervous, etc. ad nauseam.

But one of the most incredible and frightening of the phenomena happened in the spring of 1971. By that time, some of the campers had begun to come up to spend weekends on their property which was directly above us. Perhaps I should explain that the original land holding for our farm had been many acres. At the time we moved in, it consisted of only eight. The rest had been turned into campsites which were situated on the hills above and behind our house. By this time, I had been spoiled by the blissful solitude and it was always with a sense of relief that I watched the last of the campers go back to their homes.

One Sunday in May I decided to take a walk up the camp roads. The day was approaching twilight so I didn't anticipate meeting anyone. Only Lassie went with me. As we reached the top of the road, Lassie stopped dead with her ears up and every muscle at attention. Following her lead, I, too, stopped and heard the sound that had frozen her in her tracks. To my untrained ears, it sounded like a choir rehearsal. The only explanation I could think of at the time was that a group of boy scouts was practicing. The high pitched voices reminded me of the old-time castrati in Rome. The sing-song chant continued and I expected to come upon a group of singers at any moment.

As we rounded a bend in the road, however, I could no longer hear the music. Mentally shrugging, I signaled Lassie and we continued our interrupted walk. With an effort, I shook off the creepy feeling in my spine. When we reached the last cabin on the road, Lassie and I turned around to go home. Retracing our steps, we started down the steep hill. As soon as we reached the spot just before the final descent to the road, we heard the singing again. Once more, Lassie stopped and turned her head toward the mountains to the west.

This time I tried to place the sound and figure out just what it was they were singing. I was determined to be very scientific about the whole thing. The music seemed to be coming from the top of the mountain situated behind some of the camp sites and the only thing I could associate the style with was Gregorian Chant. Of course, that assumption may have been caused by my Catholic upbringing. Continuing down the road toward home, I became more and more puzzled.

Actually the incident didn't concern me too much at first. I probably wouldn't have made anything of it except for Mike's reaction. Casually, I mentioned to my blasé son, only half joking, that I thought we had ghosts up the camp road. In that tone of voice that every mother of a teenage son knows, he uttered, "Oh, Mother!" That did it! I told the whole story and found a much more receptive audience in my three daughters.

The next evening at first dark I naturally decided to go up and see if the whole thing had been my imagination. This time I was accompanied by our three dogs and my two youngest daughters. Before we reached THE PLACE, we had been joined by Beth and Pat.

After having had the night to reflect, I was sure no one would hear anything but when we reached the top of the road, sure enough, the song came through loud and clear. The girls, too, thought it was chanting and we continued walking along the road with Mary hanging onto my blouse (can't say that I blamed her). We discussed what we had heard but didn't come up with any solutions. On our way back home we halted again. As we listened, the singing stopped abruptly and, after a pause of perhaps thirty seconds, a single male voice began a monotone prayer. *It didn't sound like Latin though so I guess I can rule out Gregorian Chant.* If the singing was eerie, the prayer was worse.

Till my dying day, I'll remember the look on Pat's face. She had her pigtails pulled up over her head (I guess to hear better), her face was as white as a sheet so that her freckles stood out in bold relief and her mouth was open. In short, she looked like I felt. My skin was crawling. Needless to say, we lost no time in getting home. I told Phil about our experience and, to my surprise, he at least pretended to believe me. Every night we continued to go up the hill for the "concert" but we noticed that each time we did the sound grew more indistinct.

About a week after the day I had first heard the ghostly choir, Mike decided to investigate. He asked me to go along but, as I have always felt that discretion was the better part of valor, I politely, but firmly, declined. Matt, the worst skeptic around, agreed to go with him. Bob, surprisingly, wanted nothing to do with it. I knew Matt would love to make fools of us by proving our singing had a logical cause. As they climbed the steep slope to the top of the mountain, suddenly Matt said they shouldn't go any further. He was frightened. My intrepid son talked him into going all the way to the top.

Just as they had almost reached their goal, what sounded like a woman's scream stopped them cold. They must have broken all existing track records to get back to our house. Now, it may have been a bobcat they heard, but the fact remains that it ended our nightly concerts. I heard, from time to time, of different people hearing this mysterious singing, the last time in October of 1974 just before we left. Most people assumed there was a church nearby. There isn't–at least not one you can see.

Gradually, as the months passed, we began to realize that, at times, there was an "umbrella" descending on our house. An umbrella of fear, horror, unknown–what? I'm still not sure. On these nights the animals were restless, the birds acted crazy and no one slept. The house felt as though it sat in the center of a vacuum. Any other night I could walk down the road in the pitch dark with no qualms. On these "umbrella" nights the very atmosphere made my flesh crawl.

This sensation is not easily described. Each, in his own way, the family members felt the pressure but interpreted its results differently. There were more arguments during these times and more tears. Gradually, it began to dawn on us that the uneasiness and tension weren't self-generated but were being caused by an outside force. One by one, we came to an inward decision and when we shared our fears there was a collective sigh of relief. The pressure of each one thinking he was the only one who had made the discovery vanished.

On one such "umbrella" night I realized that Jinx, one of our cats, was not in. I have always liked all the animals in the house at night. As was my custom, I took a flashlight and went out looking for her. Briskly, I started toward the road and stopped short at the end of our house. It was as though a physical force of some type stopped me. There was nothing menacing that I could see. The breeze sighed through the pine tree with its usual comforting sound; the night was balmy and the sky clear. Across the driveway, the crabapple tree waved in the wind. Nothing unusual, no phantoms, nothing out of place, only the feeling. Why then the threat?

I had read about paranormal forces being able to force a person to a stop and, frankly, thought it was nonsense. I found out how wrong I had been. Whether I was physically restrained or only mentally, the effect was the same. I could not move.

Giving in to a feeling I can only describe as atavistic, I turned and hurried into the house, my spine tingling.

In the warm, well-let house with the sound of Simon and Garfunkel coming from the kids' stereo, my fears seemed silly and I tried again. This time my flashlight picked up two eyes over by the crabapple tree. With a deep sense of relief, I realized it could only be Jinx. Walking quietly in that direction, I talked to Jinx while keeping the flashlight pointed at the eyes the whole time. When I reached the spot the "eyes" had disappeared. A thorough search of the area revealed nothing in the grass to account for the strange phenomenon.

With my hair beginning to rise on the back of my neck, I slowly backed away, still with the flashlight glued to the spot where I had seen the "eyes". I was about eight feet away when they reappeared. This time I didn't investigate but beat an ignominious retreat to the house. Feeling a little foolish, I told no one. The story seemed too incredible. Besides, I still remembered the tone of the "Oh, Mother!"

After waiting about half an hour, my courage was at least partially restored. On sudden impulse, I decided to ask Beth to go out with me, explaining that I didn't feel right. She said it was probably because I had been alone. Leaving her homework, she took the flashlight from me and we both went out. She was about four feet ahead of me but she stopped dead at the same spot in the driveway and said, "Let's get in the house, quick. There's something wrong out here!" The only one who beat us in the house was a little black shadow named Jinx who came from the opposite side of the house.

I must admit that from that day on we respected the times the house felt "strange", the "umbrella nights", and stayed inside. We tried keeping a record of these times to see if they might fall into some sort of a pattern but soon gave up. There seemed to be no logic involved whatsoever. At this point I think I'll quote from a letter I received from Beth in October, 1974. Too bad hindsight is always better than foresight.

"The first time I noticed something strange about the family or the house it was funny 'cuz it was before Homecoming in my Sophomore year. I came home from a football game and you were doing the dishes and I walked over toward the sink and it was like a wall of hostility. You said you weren't mad but I felt something was wrong. It was funny 'cuz I remembered how you always used to sing when doing the dishes. Mary was uptight that day too. Pat was there that weekend and she kept waking me saying someone was 'breathing down her neck'. Two days after that was the first umbrella night, I remember. I don't know why I didn't remember before. I guess maybe I never let myself. I kept trying to shut everything out of my mind but it really doesn't work. I guess someday I'll tell my kids and they'll laugh and it suddenly won't seem so horrible. I think the horror started when I noticed you seldom sang anymore. Well, now you can send the men in the white coats for me."

I have read and re-read this letter over the years and am still surprised at the reaction it arouses in me. Did we miss all the clues? Did we deliberately ignore them? Or did something outside ourselves not allow us to recognize them for what they were? I hate to think such a thing is possible and yet....I continue to wonder.

Did primitive man at one time possess an ability to sense supernatural phenomena? Did we lose it in our striving for sophistication? Is it a deliberate attempt to ignore things we don't understand? Can this knowledge, or instinct perhaps, be regained?

We learn, during childhood, to interpret our "normal" feelings but, unfortunately, not our built-in instinct that warns us of "paranormal" happenings.

Chapter 4

A NEW "HAUNT"

N ow a new element entered the picture. It happened the first time when Beth and I had gone to the doctor's office for a checkup of my neck (whiplash from an accident) and her broken arm. Between us, we made a great pair. Mike stayed home with Laura and Mary. All three were in the living room when the dogs started barking. Looking out the front window, they saw a young boy of about sixteen walking along our property line in front of the house. This would be at a distance of about 20 feet.

Since he wasn't actually on our property, Mike decided to watch him instead of storming out and questioning his presence. The boy seemed not to see the house nor hear the dogs barking. As the kids watched, he walked to our pond and, for all practical purposes, disappeared in front of their eyes. I think Mike tried to convince himself that the boy had fallen in a hole although no hole exists there or that the boy somehow got out of sight without their noticing. The girls would not go along with either of these theories, though, and we were forced to admit we might have another spirit.

A short time after this incident, one of our camping neighbors and his wife were filling their water bottles at our outside faucet. We had, by this time, made friends with all the campers and they knew they were welcome to our water so long as they remembered to turn the faucet off. As they were filling the bottles, they looked up to see "the boy" near the spring house and seemingly headed toward their cabin. He was oblivious to his surroundings and didn't seem to see them at all. They didn't speak to him as they thought he was a friend of ours and felt, I suppose, a little awkward about taking water when we weren't home. However, when Grace pointed out that he was heading toward their cabin, Dick jumped into his car and made it to his property in record time.

The path the boy was taking led through an open field. In spite of this fact, there was no sign of him. Grace went to the upstairs window of their red, barn-shaped cabin from which you could see for miles. Dick covered every inch of the camping area in his car. Neither of them found any sign of the boy. Dick is a lieutenant in the police department of a city near Buffalo and a trained observer. Neither of them had known about the previous sighting.

Strangely enough, though the couple saw the boy at the same time, their descriptions of his clothes were different. Dick swore he wore jeans while Grace was just as sure his slacks were chinos. This is the first time since the encounter with the "black man" that we realized that descriptions of psychic phenomena often vary even if seen at the same time.

Looking back, I can see a gradual build-up of power. What kind of power? Again, I must confess, I don't know. I only know we became increasingly aware of "something". I told Phil how we felt and was prepared for his derision. I was surprised to find, although he didn't fully appreciate what was happening, still he didn't make fun of our feelings.

How were Phil and I getting along? Not too well, I'm afraid. He seldom came home but spent the week nights at my mother and father's house and only some weekends with us. It was almost as though he didn't have a family. In fact, it was getting so the kids and I were just as well pleased when he stayed away. His presence always caused tension in the house and things were much more peaceful when he wasn't there. I don't know if he felt the strangeness in the house. We had reached the point where vital communications had broken down.

Due to the pressure the kids and I were feeling in the house, I no longer had the energy to indulge his tantrums and, I guess, he resented it. He had always been a drinker but now the saloon had become more important than his home. The kids and I were under abnormal pressure and it took abnormal strength to withstand it. I had no energy left to try to save my disintegrating marriage. Sadly, I had begun to cease caring.

In addition to our other problems, our financial situation was going steadily downhill and nothing we did seemed to help. The house was not to blame for this difficulty. Phil was bringing home less and less money and his explanations didn't always make sense. My trust in him began eroding.

On two different occasions I tried working. The first job didn't pay enough and was really out of my line. The job was with an Olean department store and I worked as an assistant to the bookkeeper and a relief saleslady. I'm afraid I'll never make a salesperson. Before a month was up, I had quit.

The second job was with the County Board of Cooperational Educational Services (B.O.C.E.S) and I enjoyed it. I had to give that one up, though, when my neck started to bother me. The whiplash I had suffered in my auto accident in 1971 came back with a vengeance. Though I had periods of remission sometimes lasting three or four weeks, one morning I'd wake up and be, literally, unable to raise my head from the pillow without using my hands. When I left my job in June of 1973 I thought perhaps I could recover over the summer by working in my garden and just taking it easy. I didn't know then that the summer would turn into a living nightmare. *I had another reason for leaving the job as well. One day, I reluctantly left Mary home alone while I went to work. She had a bad cold and was feeling pretty sick. As she rested, a loud pounding started at the back door. The dogs went crazy and were barking wildly and jumping at the door. The pounding went on. Mary, heart in mouth, came downstairs. The man she saw out the kitchen window looked scary to her. She called me, panic-stricken. The door was locked but she didn't trust the lock. The barking of the dogs seemed to have no affect on the "caller". I jumped in my car and headed for home. It seemed an interminable drive. I was imagining all sorts of scenes when I reached home. By the time I got there, the caller had disappeared leaving only a tearful, terrified young girl and three very disturbed dogs. She spent the rest of the day at BOCES with me.*

In writing this book, I have become aware of some facts that surprised me. For one thing, I didn't react as I would have predicted, nor did the rest of the family. I found out I didn't mind stranger's doubts about our veracity so much as long as those we loved believed and supported us. I have always marveled at the heroines of gothic novels who stay in "haunted houses" and yet, we did not run until staying became unthinkable. My whole outlook on life, including religion, took an awful beating and proved a need for a complete revamping of my beliefs. I don't know if I'd ever be comfortable in that house again and, yet, I'm tempted to return. The house still holds a tremendous charm and appeal for me. In spite of everything, some of the happiest days of my life were spent in that house.

My reasons for writing this book are myriad. Number one, I think, is that it acts as a kind of cathartic to get rid of some of the tensions which had been built up over the period of our residence and afterwards. Sometimes I bitterly resent what happened to us since it deeply affected every member of the family and all of those close to us. Number two, since suffering the trauma of having people laughing, doubting and snickering behind our backs, I want them to know how proud I am of my family. I don't know many who could have stood up to the extraordinary pressures they had to face. Three, I would like people to know why I let the newspaper publish our story. And four, I want to thank, publicly, the many people who called and wrote to assure us that they did believe our incredible story and the surprising number who offered to help.

I am especially grateful to the teenagers in town who never lost faith in us; helped in every way they could and defended us even though, in doing so, they sometimes got into trouble. Our families, both Phil's and mine, and, of course, Father Al, deserve a special thanks since, without their support, we could not have held on as long as we did. Perhaps I am also writing to convince myself that what happened actually **did** happen.

No one seemed to realize that our family was the first to doubt; our family was the first to question; our family was the first to seek some rational explanation to some very irrational happenings. I am also using the book to bring some semblance of order to events that seemed, at times, to flow together. I can't possibly tell every little thing that happened because, after a while, everything took on a dreamlike quality and, unless an event were written down when it happened, we tended to forget it. We also began to accept as normal, things which were decidedly abnormal. Believe me, that's a danger signal.

Now, I will begin the story. Did you think I already had? Those were only the preliminaries. Now, to begin. I have decided to tell our story in semi-diary form so that I can sort out not only the events but our changes of attitudes as well. The people involved besides our family will be identified as they appear. I am using first names only so as to avoid any embarrassment to those involved.

At the point where the story begins our family consisted of: Me, of course; at the time of the story I was 37 years old. Phil, my husband, was 39. Mike, who at 17, was very conscious of his age and took his increasing responsibilities seriously when his father wasn't home. Because he considered himself short at 5'7", he tried to make up for his lack of height with a keen sense of humor and a compulsive, perpetual motion. Beth, 16, with her long brown hair and laughing brown eyes, was my right hand. We are very much alike and, without her, I doubt I could have withstood the ordeal. No matter how bad things got I could always talk it over with Beth and then we'd laugh together. Laura, 12, was the only one of the kids who inherited my blue eyes. She was an eternal optimist and, so we've come to believe, the most psychic in the family. All her life I had considered Laura fey. Perhaps I was right. Mary, 11, had brown eyes and the most beautiful wavy blonde hair that gets lighter as the sun touches it. Poor Mary, she was in a state of constant fear because her room seemed the most troubled. At 11, or any other age for that matter, one shouldn't be expected to deal with the paranormal.

We also had the following animals at this point: our three dogs–Lassie (a collie), Julie (terrier mix) and Peanuts (a German Shepherd and St. Bernard mix); two cats–Fluffy (part tabby and part angora) and Jinx (the classic black cat); two raccoons–Gypsy and her son, Jasper; one guinea pig–Barney; two parakeets–Pixie and Jingles; and our pet skunk–Dolly (de-scented). I will ask you to read the event following with an open mind because THEY ARE ALL TRUE!!

Chapter 5

Friday—June 29, 1973

What a beautiful day it was today! I could feel the promise of a good summer coming up. Laura had to have her eyes examined in Olean so Phil offered to take her while I went for my usual visit to the doctor. I had no idea the results of whiplash would last so long. In fact, to my embarrassment, I have always considered whiplash victims to be malingerers. Poetic justice. I found out I was wrong the hard way. Serves me right, I guess. The rest of the kids decided to go along with Phil into town. Since their father isn't home very often, I'm always glad when they have some time with him. In their absence, I had some time to myself, a rare thing. Since our house is usually filled with kids, I decided to enjoy my solitude and read in peace for a change.

I am a voracious reader who scans labels on packages in the absence of any more thrilling reading. I settled down on the couch in the living room with a big sigh when suddenly I heard what sounded like a big pile of newspapers fall. Since I had just finished straightening the newspapers piled on a desk on the front porch, I assumed I hadn't done a good job. Reluctantly, I got up from my comfortable seat and went to the porch to check.

The porch was one of my favorite places. The windows still enclose it and will remain in place until summer makes its final appearance. They overlook a panorama of magnificent trees still shaking off their winter sleep. Taking a moment to enjoy the panorama, I saw beautiful scenery but no fallen newspapers. They were still piled just as I had left them. Puzzled, I searched the whole house and could find no papers fallen anywhere.

Weird! I thought. Finally, I shrugged mentally and went back to my book.

I had barely gotten settled when, without any warning the window directly in front of me and at a distance of about ten feet, slammed shut. The windows in this century-plus old house are ancient and have no sash cords so when one of them falls the whole house shakes. I jumped three feet in the air. When I looked, the window **had not fallen!** Again, I checked the house but, again, could find no cause for the sound. All the windows that had been open to let in the warm air were still open. I was puzzled and more than a little disturbed. Still, it must have a natural explanation. Mustn't it? Resolutely, I decided to ignore the whole thing and get ready for my appointment with the doctor. So much for peaceful reading!

Because of the absurdity of the occurrence, I decided not to mention the episode to Phil. Besides, he'd probably think I was imagining things. Am I?

Monday-July 2, 1973

In spite of my new awareness caused by the strange sounds last Friday, I am pleased to report that nothing further has happened. Perhaps naïvely, I am, therefore, going to attribute the whole thing to natural causes or an overactive imagination. However, don't ask me what natural causes and don't ask me how an imagination can cause you to hear a noise as loud as that one. I hope I'm not whistling in the dark.

Today, as usual, Phil left for work at about 9 p.m. and everything seemed normal. He has been spending more time at home lately and I have hopes that this is a good sign. Beth, Mike and I are the only ones home. Laura and Mary have gone to Buffalo to spend the weekend with my mother and father. Our evening was pleasant and unspectacular. We went to bed about 11 and I dropped right off to sleep.

At about 3:30 in the morning a scream coming from downstairs sent me leaping from my bed. I grabbed my bathrobe and dodged Lassie, Julie and the two cats to get down the stairway. The stairs are steep and I am always very cautious when

I descend. I managed to get one arm in my robe correctly but didn't realize I put the other sleeve on inside out so that the robe crossed in back. All the way down the stairs I tried frantically to fix my robe. Maybe my preoccupation with the robe kept me from becoming too panic stricken at the screams still echoing from Beth's room.

There were no lights on in the house and I stumbled over furniture as I fumbled in the pitch darkness for a light switch. In the country there are no street lights and the darkness is absolute. I finally managed to calm my shaking hands long enough to find a lamp and light it. Anxiously, I looked in Beth's room and saw her lying with her hands pressed to her eyes. Peanuts was offering her a shoe–his idea of a pacifier.

When I finally got her calmed down, she told me that something had attacked her although she didn't seem too sure of what it was. Fluffy had been sleeping on her bed but left when Beth got up to get a drink of water a little before 3:30. She was no sooner back in bed when "something" landed on her stomach. It took her eyes a second to accustom themselves to the dark, so all she could make out was a shadow resembling a cat. Suddenly, it went for her face. Instinctively, she swung her arm to knock it off. It was soft and furry, like Fluffy, but smaller–more the size of Jinx. It wasn't until she realize that the "thing" didn't hit the floor that she started to scream.

Since I knew both cats had been upstairs when she screamed, I knew it had been neither of them. Peanuts is part German Shepherd and part St. Bernard so size alone ruled him out, as it did the other two dogs. Besides, none of our animals would have attacked any of us. I made Beth come to my room for the remainder of the night. As we climbed the stairs, I could feel goose bumps belatedly rising on my arms. Settling quickly into bed, we talked of everything but the subject uppermost in our minds. Thankfully, dawn brought relief and blessed sleep.

Tuesday–July 3, 1973

Well, he did it again! This morning, with superb understatement, Mike sleepily asked: "Was Beth crying last night or something?" When I told him what had happened, he couldn't have been more blasé, giving me the distinct impression that he didn't believe us. To add to the mystery, I found what appeared to be animal excreta in front of Beth's door this morning. At first I was angry with the cats but, since I knew they were well trained and fastidious, I found their "goof" hard to believe. Besides, the matter was grayish green and slimy but odorless. *It resembled greasy modeling clay.*

As I cleaned it up it occurred to me that I had seen the same substance once before. Belatedly, the light began to dawn. Beth had broken her arm in April and had screamed the same way one night while she still had her cast on. She had swung her arm, the one with the cast, and it hit her dressing table. At the time, she could give me no explanation. Now I questioned her about it again. The last time she saw the "thing" come at her from behind the bed, she thought she was dreaming. The fear of being thought foolish kept her from telling us what had happened. So this wasn't the first time. The day following the first incident, I had found the same "message" near the entrance to her room and grumblingly blamed the poor cats. Now what are we dealing with?

Phil only half believed us when he got home and probably thought that Beth was dreaming. But he hadn't seen her face. I also knew she hadn't been asleep when it happened. As so often happens with mothers, it had drifted through my sleep that Beth had left her bed and I half heard the water running in the bathroom. That's probably why I woke up so easily.

Mike won't be home tonight. He and his friends are leaving early in the morning for the amusement park at Crystal Beach in Canada so they're spending the night together in one of their houses. Phil will be here, though, so maybe nothing will happen. I don't know why I think that or why I should have to.

Wednesday–July 4, 1973

At least it was quiet last night. Maybe the whole thing was our overactive imaginations. Phil and I came down to have breakfast about 10 o'clock this morning. To get to the stairway

Phil had to pass by Mary's room so I would assume if anything had been wrong in there he would have noticed. He doesn't miss much. Failing that, I myself would have seen anything out of the ordinary.

After breakfast, I went back upstairs to get dressed. I glanced in at Mary's room as I passed and saw her milk glass lamp on the floor. The base was about three feet from her nightstand while the heavy glass chimney was right at the doorway, about seven feet away. The bulb had shattered all over the room. I was stunned.

The lamp has fallen before and the sound echoed through the house. It is very heavy. Beth sleeps directly under Mary's room and would have heard even a light sound, especially since we have become overly sensitive to anything out of the ordinary. Not only that, but I had seen Beth move the lamp on the nightstand the night before. As is the habit in this animal-oriented home, she caught the cord behind the stand so none of the animals could trip over it. Beth had been getting Mary's seldom-used night light which was in the shape of the Infant of Prague. As a family, we liked to sleep in the dark but I didn't blame Beth for wanting a night light. Before too long, we would all become addicted to night lights and would not be ashamed to admit it.

Phil tried to explain away the lamp incident but I couldn't buy it. Beth and I painstakingly picked up all the fine shards of glass from the bulb so no one would get cut. The floor was completely clear when we left the room. I don't believe I went upstairs again that day. Since Phil and I had disagreed on what was happening, I'm afraid I was rather annoyed with him when he left for work tonight.

After Phil left, Beth's boyfriend, Jeff, was reluctant to leave us alone in the house. He, too, had sensed the change in the atmosphere. No matter what we were doing, he'd suddenly break out in goose bumps about dusk. He claimed it was his Indian blood. I was glad he stayed until late because we could all sense an alien, unfriendly aura in the house. It was the same sensation we had when the "umbrella" used to descend on the house, only now it was **inside**!

Mike finally came in, tired after his long drive, his eyes sore from trying to see on a rain-soaked highway. Early summer in

New York State often produced heavy and unexpected rainfalls, usually accompanied by spectacular lightning. Since Mike was home, Jeff finally felt it was safe to leave.

After Jeff went home, we tried to tell Mike why Jeff had been so concerned. My unruffled son was completely disinterested in the incidents of the day. He was too tired to listen and just wanted the lights out so he could get some sleep. We were so relieved he was home, we were only too happy to oblige. I went upstairs and started to get into bed when I spotted something lying on Mary's floor. Without thinking, I moved to pick it up. It took a few seconds before it dawned on me that it was the Ace of Spades I held in my hand. Since the only deck of cards we possessed was kept downstairs in a drawer, I had no idea where it could have come from.

Creeping quietly downstairs, feeling cold and frightened, I knocked on Beth's door. Careful not to wake Mike, I asked her if she had noticed anything on the floor when we finished cleaning up the glass. She confirmed what I already knew and was appalled when she saw the card.

Recalling this incident later, it is incredible to me to think that all I did was put the card under my alarm clock with the intention of showing it to Phil in the morning. Then I went to bed. Why didn't it occur to me that I was sleeping alone upstairs not ten feet from where we had been having some very strange disturbances?

The alarm clock said it was about 4 o'clock in the morning and, apparently, I woke at the first sound. A quivering voice was calling, "Ma!" and I knew it was Mike. When I answered, he asked me to come downstairs. Being half asleep, I was reluctant to leave my comfortable bed but finally got up. Donning my bathrobe, I went downstairs, reached his door and stopped short.

His chess set was scattered from one end of the room to the other and his Battleship game was lying on top of him. I said, "My God, what happened?" All he could say was, "I'm not getting out of this bed until you come into the room." I stepped in immediately. He decided to sleep on the couch for the rest of the night and kept reminding Beth not to turn out her night light (as if he had to tell her!).

Thursday-July 5, 1973

Would you believe it? This morning I went to look for the card under my clock and it wasn't there. I finally found it on Mary's dresser. Phil's solution–I must have walked in my sleep. I have never walked in my sleep in my life. Come to think of it, I wasn't getting a whole lot of sleep lately. When would I have time to walk? I have given up trying to convince Phil. I don't even blame him. In the morning I get up and see the sun shining, hear the birds singing and wonder how I could have possibly imagined such nonsense. Yet, I know it did happen and the impossibility of it is overwhelming. I feel reality slipping sideways under me.

Beth discovered a burn on her leg this morning. It was definitely not there last night. When she spoke of it, Mike looked shocked and then said he had a similar burn appear on **his** leg about a week before but hadn't mentioned it because it didn't hurt. Beth's did hurt and she developed a permanent scar from it.

By this time, Mike had mentally replayed the events of the night before. His logical mind didn't like what he was telling it. There is a wide, room-long shelf over his bed. On it, he keeps books, games, magazines and what have you. Like any mother, I had warned him time and again about the precarious pile of slick magazines perched on top of his games but the **magazines didn't fall**. His chess set, which was on the very bottom of a large pile, fell on his chest and woke him up. Sleepily pushing it off to the floor, he turned over to go back to sleep. About five minutes later, his Battleship game, which had been on top of the chess game, fell. That was when he called me.

The magazines were still piled on the shelf, still precarious but unmoved while the games beneath them lay all over the floor. Since Mike prides himself on being logical and this was completely illogical, he was absolutely convinced that something strange was happening in the house. He kept shouting, "But they fell on me!" All Beth and I said was, "Join the club." Neither of us felt the least bit callous.

From being a scoffing disbeliever, Mike has become a bundle of nerves. Suddenly, he was frantic to find some believable explanation. Right away, he insisted we visit the town historian so the three of us stopped in on the way to the post office. Strangely enough, a man who had been born in a house which used to stand next to ours was visiting in her kitchen. In fact, this man was a descendent of the original owners of the property, or so he claimed. When the lady of the house asked if anything strange ever happened up at the house when he lived there he just shook his head and refused to comment.

There was another man there at the time who started what was to become the common hobby of making fun of us. I can't understand people who jeer at something because it's different or unusual. We were groping in the dark, asking for help, and he laughed. I hope he enjoyed himself at our expense and I hope nothing similar ever happens to him. He couldn't take it!

Of course, Phil thinks the boxes falling was just an accident but Mike has become a staunch and confirmed ally. It's not just two giddy women now. Mike does not panic easily and he tried to tell Phil how frightened he had been. Actually, it isn't only the incident itself which is unnerving enough, but the atmosphere in the area of the incident. It's very hard to describe but is a clinging, cold feeling. There's an electric-like charge in the air. However, after the encounter with Mike's doubts, I have come to the conclusion that you must go through an experience like this yourself before you can fully appreciate or believe it so I didn't insist. Besides, it wouldn't have helped if I had.

We talked it over, Mike, Beth and I, and have decided we will not discuss the strange events of the past few days but will try to keep the atmosphere light and see if that might help. At this point, affected by Phil's doubts, we had somehow come to the mistaken conclusion that we were, at least partially, to blame for the weirdness. After Phil left for work, the three of us sat watching the Walton's on TV and having Pepsi and potato chips. We had no discussion of anything more profound that whether to watch Kung Fu after the Walton's or try something else for a change. It was a night like so many others with nothing to mark it as unique.

On the front wall in the living room, directly over the vinyl reclining chair on which I was sitting, were pictures of the four kids. I had hung their First Communion pictures and, alongside them, their latest school pictures and the effect was very interesting. Suddenly Mike asked what was stuck in Mary's picture. When I looked up, I felt my scalp crawl. There was a clear plastic letter opener balanced in Mary's picture, making it look as though she had been stabbed. The picture, thank God, was not punctured. A sense of complete unreality filled me as I told them what it was.

Beth immediately burst into tears and said, "Why is it picking on Mary? She isn't even here!" Our brave attempts at lightness crumbled and proved false in that instant. Mike was the first one to move. Angrily snatching the opener, he broke it in several pieces and threw it into the kitchen. Each lost in his own thoughts; we sat quietly for some minutes.

Abruptly, Mike made us realize that our thoughts were almost identical. I was frantically asking myself if I had "flipped" and might have done this crazy thing myself and not remembered it. One look at Beth's stricken face told me she was thinking the same thing. Mike cleared the air with his next words. "One thing–we know it's not one of us–we have more imagination!" With considerable relief, I knew he was right.

Rather shakily, he suggested that we all sleep in the same room, at least for the night. He felt that whatever "it" was seemed to be trying to separate us. One of the indications of how frightened and off-balance we had become was when Mike said, "I am a seventeen year old boy about to ask my sixteen year old sister to walk to the bathroom with me." Beth agreed as long as he'd wait outside the door while she was in the bathroom. Only those with teenagers can fully appreciate the panic contained in those remarks.

Together, we went upstairs to bed. Beth and I slept in my bed and Mike set up a cot alongside. I wish there were some way I could convey the horror I felt as I lay in my own bed with my own kids, surrounded by my own pets and listened to the sound of men's heavy footsteps downstairs walking from one end of the house to the other all night long. Whoever it was, or whatever, was wearing hard-soled boots. At least that's what it sounded like. I found myself wishing he'd take them off. Does it sound as though I was overtired? I felt weighed down by *the house and its persecution*. Would this fatigue impair my ability to act? I hope not. There are too many indications that we must keep our wits about us and keep strong. I must recover!

I should mention that none of the animals seemed to hear the footsteps but Julie and Fluffy are showing an increasing reluctance to come in the house at night. At least some of the pets would ordinarily have slept downstairs but this night they all crowded into my room, close together as if for moral support.

Friday–July 6, 1973

I guess Mike must have mentioned our problems to some of his friends because Craig asked to spend the night and "chase our noises". I don't know if he's making fun of us, wants to psych us into believing he's chased our "spooks" or truly wants to help. Craig, although I don't know him too well, always acts like a quiet, pleasant boy and I like him. At any rate, we spent a quiet evening watching television and talking of nothing in particular. None of us mentioned the troubles we have been having.

Because it was Friday night, Phil didn't have to go to work. We went up to bed after the evening news was over at 11:30. However, no sooner had we settled down than Mike came to our door and said quietly, "Dad, that boy is outside again." There was no need to tell us what "boy" he meant. Phil had his clothes on and was outside before I could get my bathrobe on.

Craig had been on his way to bed when, passing our back kitchen door, he chanced to look out. Just then he saw the "boy" walking past our spring house. He didn't know anything about that particular spirit and shouted to Mike that "some kid" had just gone through our yard. This is highly suspicious when it's near midnight and the house is about four miles from town.

Craig must have been rather confused when Mike and Phil ran all through the yard and surrounding fields trying to find a boy he had been told "walked around here". He kept saying to anyone who would listen, "If he walks around here where does he live? Why is he walking around at midnight?" I finally told him that we thought it might be a ghost. At this, he immediately began apologizing to everyone saying, "I didn't mean to see him, honest. I'm sorry–I didn't mean to see him." It took quite a while to calm him down. Well, someone else has seen our young phantom. I sure wish I would.

Saturday–July 7, 1973

Since it seems as though we are unable to cope with the events of the past couple of weeks ourselves, I called my mother on Thursday to see if she could reach my cousin, Father Bob. I had been unable to get anyone to bless the house before this and thought perhaps if he blessed it the house would settle down. Am I being naïve again? She couldn't reach Father Bob but assured me that he would be at the family reunion on Sunday.

I hadn't been sure up to this point whether I was going to attend. The annual reunion is being held on Grand Island, north of Buffalo, and is quite a long drive for us. However, clinging to the hope that Father Bob could help us, I decided to make the drive. Mike planned to ask Brenda to go with him and Beth asked Pat. Pat and her family had moved to a town near Buffalo when her mother remarried and she was in town visiting her grandmother. We made all the preparations for our picnic/reunion and determined to enjoy ourselves.

Sunday–July 8, 1973

What a beautiful day for a reunion! The air was clear, the sun bright and the weather hot. The kids decided to take their swim suits. The park is situated right on the Niagara River, not too far from my brother, Martin's, house and it has a good beach. Mary, who with Laura, has been visiting my mother and father, decided to come home with us after the picnic. Laura wanted to stay in Buffalo a few more days.

When I called mum about Father Bob, I told her all about our problem and asked her to see if the kids had seen my plastic letter opener. Neither of them knew what I was talking about. I thought I was the only one who knew where it had been before it appeared in Mary's picture but I was wrong. Even I hadn't known!

When I quit my job at BOCES, I put the opener, a freebie from Fuller Brush, in a bag and stored it in the front closet. I checked after the incident with the picture and couldn't find the bag. It was a few days later that I found it in the upstairs bedroom closet. I must have moved it with some other things and not realized it. So, how had the opener gotten in Mary's picture? With all the strange things that were going on, I really didn't blame the girls for not wanting to come home.

Midday at the park was really hot and we were plagued by little black flies but I think everyone had a good time. I was really upset, however, when I discovered the large diamond in my engagement ring was missing. For an hour, we searched but trying to find something like that in a park is impossible. I still have dreams of some child finding it and playing with the piece of "glass".

I hated the thought of telling Phil about my ring. He's had quite enough shocks lately without adding this one. Because he had to work in the evening, he decided not to come today but planned on spending the day resting.

Father Bob was late and arrived just as we were about to give up and pack our things to go home. He listened sympathetically to my story and promised to come to the house as soon as possible. He confessed he might not be able to help, though, and thought that I might have to get in touch with someone who "does that sort of thing". I guess medicine isn't the only field with areas of specialization.

Since we had a long drive home, we left rather early. I asked mum and dad to come down for a visit. Mum still had her cast on, so she said they would come down on Tuesday. That would give her a day to rest up. Mary came home with us, although with some reluctance, but Laura decided to stay until mum and dad came down.

All of us were tired after our long day so I suggested that Pat and Brenda spend the night. The three older girls slept in the living room, Mike in his bedroom and I in my room upstairs. The worst part of a picnic to me is putting everything away when you get home. I remember so clearly putting the charcoal lighter out on the back porch!

Monday–July 9, 1973

Well, my first surprise this morning was finding the charcoal lighter in the bathroom next to the wastebasket *and uncomfortably close to the water heater*. For a moment I was completely disoriented. I could see myself taking that lighter out to the back porch. Yet, here it was in the bathroom. Impossible! When the girls got up, Beth found a tear-shaped burn about an inch and a half long in my good criss-cross curtains. I had just washed them the week before so I knew the burn hadn't been there.

To top it all off, one of the leaves of my philodendron plant was also burned. Alarmingly enough, the burns were the same shape as the one Beth had on her leg. They looked like they had been caused by drops of acid. First there were the burns and then the lighter fluid. I couldn't figure it out. Certainly, it seemed as though something were threatening us with fire. How does it know that fire is one of my greatest fears?

When Phil came home from work, I reluctantly told him about the diamond and, thank God, he wasn't as upset as I thought he'd be. It's our 18th *wedding* anniversary today, too. What an anniversary present!

Brenda went home this morning but Pat decided to stay over another night. Soon, she'll have to go back home to Buffalo and she and Beth are trying to catch up on all the gossip.

Mike noticed a very disturbing atmosphere in his room when he was going to bed tonight and asked if he could sleep on the couch. I wasn't about to order him to sleep where he felt uncomfortable. Pat slept on a cot at the side of Beth's bed. All night long, she kept waking Mike, frightened and anxious to talk. As they talked, they both heard footsteps coming from the kitchen *about three uncomfortable yards away.* When Mike assured her it must be one of the animals, she insisted he check. Neither of them slept much after finding out there were no animals in the kitchen.

Tuesday—July 10, 1973

All our company came today. Mum and dad arrived with Laura and then, around supper time, Father Bob, his mother and his sister, June, showed up. Yesterday I tried to find out the name and address of a couple who had lectured at St. Bonaventure University in October on psychic phenomena but the priest who could give me the information was always out of the office. I tried again today and got their name but was advised that I should instead call Father Alphonsus at the University. He studies psychic phenomena and helps out in cases like ours. Here, I thought we were unique. I immediately put in a call to Father but, he, too, was out. It's certainly my day for striking out. Hopes rising, I left a message with the switchboard operator and prayed he'd call back soon.

As soon as mum and dad arrived with Laura, as always, I felt relieved. A remnant of childhood, perhaps, but I think even grownups, in times of great peril, call their mothers. We talked over all that had happened and came to no conclusions. They were horrified and rather outraged that anything would bother us like this. They, too, couldn't wait until Father Alphonsus returned my call, I don't know what we expected–magic, I guess.

After Father Bob arrived, we ate a picnic supper. Our yard was perfect for that. The view of the surrounding countryside and rolling landscape made everyone enjoy themselves. After eating, Father blessed the house and then we sat in the living room and went over the events again. My aunt thinks it has something to do with the devil but I don't agree. Of course, the fact that I don't believe in the devil as a viable entity might have something to do with my doubt. *Besides, if there is a "devil" I think he probably has more important things to do than harass a family in a small town.*

As I looked out the window and watched dusk creeping over the mountains, I had a sudden, overwhelming feeling of foreboding. I knew the atmosphere in the house was unchanged and that the blessing had not helped. As my heart sank down to my shoes, I realized that Father Bob was watching me and sensed what I felt. Like a child, I guess I expected all our troubles to disappear miraculously after the blessing. Of course, that's akin to superstition but that's what I hoped. As they left, Father Bob said, "I don't know if I did you any good but I didn't do you any harm." I wish I could have reassured him that his blessing had worked but I couldn't. *At the time we didn't know that what we were dealing with required much more than a blessing to get rid of it.*

I will sleep the sleep of exhaustion tonight and I think if the devil himself shows up I won't know it–or care.

Wednesday–July 11, 1973

I'm always glad when mum and dad visit. We lived in their lower flat before we left Buffalo. The kids and I had been accustomed to being able to pop upstairs for a quick word *or a snack.* Today, we had a pleasant time just visiting and I began to hope, as usual, that whatever had been here had left. Perhaps Father's blessing had helped. In the evening, I suddenly became utterly exhausted and went in to lie on Beth's bed. Mum, dad and the girls were watching TV in the living room right outside the bedroom door. I had Dolly, the skunk, with me and we both lay down and drifted into a light sleep, Dolly lying on my stomach.

I had only slept a few minutes when I woke to an Arctic cold in the room. Beth had been complaining that her room, ordinarily the warmest room in the house, was icy cold lately. As I lay there I felt my fingers getting stiff and even the warmth of Dolly's body didn't help. It must have been because I just woke up that it took me so long to realize that what I was feeling was not a normal cold. This cold seemed to drain the warmth from the inside of my body. *It was as though icy fingers were raking the lining of my stomach.*

All I could think of was that my mother would be sleeping in this room very shortly and she had a broken leg. Finally, I got up and said, "Mum, you'd better not sleep in here tonight–it's too cold." She knew right away what I meant but said it would be all right. I joined them in the living room and after a few minutes saw mum go into Beth's room. She heartily agreed–it was cold! Seeing the look on her face, I knew that she realized what was causing the sudden drop in temperature. For some reason, her knowing helped me to attain at least a semblance of calm.

At that moment, Beth, who had just washed her hair, went to the bathroom to comb it out when the faucet in the bathroom sink suddenly went on full force. She let out a yelp and returned, laughing nervously, saying that it could at least have waited until she had wanted to wash her hands.

Just then Mike came home with his friend, Randy C, who was going to spend the night. This was nothing new. Since we moved in, we had a constant parade of kids spending the night. I have gotten used to it and probably wouldn't know what to do if they quit coming. Our house is so isolated that it's difficult to carry on a social life without this hospitality.

The minute I saw Randy, I felt, with wonder, that the atmosphere in the house was lifting. I told mum I thought the bedroom would be all right now and, when she checked, sure enough, the room was slowly warming. From this day on, Randy became known as my "Spook Chaser".

Thursday–July 12, 1973

Today I got a call from Father Alphonsus. He said if he could get a car he'd stop over. It was afternoon when he finally arrived. The back roads in our area had confused him and he had passed the turnoff to our house. Once that mistake is made, there is nothing to do but to continue on to the "Flats" and turn around. The main road is narrow and, just past our street, has a mountain towering on one side and a steep drop-off on the other. At least he made it. To say we were anxiously awaiting his arrival would be a gross understatement. When we explained what had happened, he didn't act surprised nor did he doubt a word of what we said. He just sat puffing on his pipe, his eyes half closed in thought, absorbing everything we said.

His quiet acceptance of our incredible tale made us feel much better. Up to this point we all felt cut off from the world and I was vaguely afraid we were some kind of freaks. He asked permission to come up in the evening and, of course, I readily gave it. The first, tentative diagnosis he gave us was that we might have poltergeists. I had heard of such things but never expected to play host to them. Although some of the incidents didn't seem to fit in, still it was an interesting theory. *Learning later that "poltergeist" activity is usually caused by energy generated by adolescents, I can see why Father latched onto the idea. He was in for a big surprise.*

Father Al returned in the evening and I knew he was dying to see the "boy". My brother, Gordon, was visiting and so was Craig. They went with Mike, Laura and Father for a walk around the area. Of course, they found nothing. Father talked with me for quite a while and I learned a little bit about this incredible thing they call psychic phenomena. I wish mum and dad hadn't had to leave this afternoon. I know they would have enjoyed his explanation.

When he left us, we felt much better and I had some hope for the future. At least we had a friend, someone who believed us. When something incredible happens, it's comforting when someone with authority can reduce it to even semi-scientific facts.

I came to know over the next confusing months that Father Al's own calmness and his ability to convey that serenity to others was, perhaps, his greatest gift. It took me a while to realize that, while he verbally reassured us that there would be no more troubles after he'd gone, it was more a placebo than a cure. Sometimes it worked. Mostly, it didn't.

Friday–July 13, 1973

Well, it's Friday the 13th! It should be interesting living in this house on Friday the 13th. Last week I had told another camping neighbor about the happenings because I knew she belonged to a club interested in the supernatural. Charmaine was a former nun and I hoped she might know of some solution to our problem. Later that evening she had called long distance from her home in Buffalo.

Surprising me, she asked that each of us write something on pieces of paper and seal them in separate envelopes. We were to put some code on the outside of the envelope so only we would know to whom each of the envelopes belonged. Her friend, Maureen, knew a psychic who performed psychometry and they thought they could find out who in the family was providing the energy for the supposed poltergeists. Charmaine and Maureen were to come down and pick up the envelopes and let us know the results as soon as possible.

This was becoming quite an education. Did you ever try to think of something to write on a slip of paper? It took the kids some time to come up with appropriate prose. The fact that no one would be reading them didn't seem to matter at all. Even Phil cooperated.

Saturday–July 14, 1973

Friday the 13th had proven to be no different than any other day and, indeed, had turned out quieter than most. Charmaine and Maureen came today for the envelopes. Maureen, who belongs to a serious psychic study group, advised us to surround ourselves with "white light". It was the first time (but not the last) I had ever heard that term. This is a way of saying "God's grace" and is supposed to be a little easier to master. We were told to picture the house and then white light surrounding it. It seemed easy enough and we were willing to try just about anything at this point.

In the evening we gathered together, the kids and I, and tried our luck with the "white light". I felt childishly pleased with myself when I pictured the house and even more pleased when I saw a bright white aura surrounding it. My pleasure turned to panic, however, when the vision suddenly changed, seemingly of its own volition. Rather than be alarmed, I was surprised and very puzzled.

My house was covered with leaves. They must have been oak leaves because they resembled tiny hands. There was a tree between the two living room windows and a tree in back by the utility room window. Both were growing up over the house and completely obscuring it. The leaves reaching out to cover the windows seemed to be growing out of the roof itself. I was horrified. I blurted out, "My house is covered with trees!"

Mike said scornfully, "Mom, you know our house has no trees around it!" Nevertheless, I couldn't get the picture out of my mind. I closed my eyes again and saw a giant root snake from under the soil again. It was like watching a movie. I was not controlling my vision–my vision was controlling me. With trepidation, I mentioned the irrationality of my mental picture. Sensibly, Mike suggested, "Maybe you've got the wrong house."

This made as much sense as anything else so I looked inward again. It was the wrong house, or at least it looked different from the house we were living in now. This house also had two differently slanted roofs but they were both on the same level where only one half of our house had two floors. The roof on the house in the vision was black, our roof was green. I felt an incredible sense of relief, although I can't explain why. I still wonder whose house I saw.

On one of our drives through the surrounding countryside a few weeks later, the kids and I saw a house that duplicated the one in my vision. It was deserted and looked like it had been so for a long time. Whose house was it? And why had I seen it? *Was it a vision of the past or the future? The answer scares me, whichever it is.*

Tuesday–July 17, 1973

Thank God, it was comparatively quiet over the weekend and, as usual, we all hoped the peace would continue. Laura and Mary each had a friend over for the weekend so I was relieved when nothing happened. The kids' guests weren't, though. Visitors always want to see something. I guess they're all hoping that something weird will happen so they can brag about it. Don't they realize how frightening it is? I guess our fame or infamy, as the case may be, is spreading. I don't know what this thing can do but I don't want to put anyone in danger. *It's bad enough that our family is forced to face the unknown daily without dragging others into it.*

Charmaine and Maureen brought the envelopes back today with the news that I was supposedly the power that was enabling the events in the house to occur and Mary was supposed to be the channel of that power. This seems rather odd because Mary wasn't even in the house when most of the events were taking place. Since this whole thing is completely new to me, I don't really understand what they mean. I am, I guess, supposed to have some psychic power. Anyway, they said my envelope jumped right out of Wally's (the psychic) hand after getting uncomfortably hot when he held it. I found this hard to believe. Is my skepticism showing?

I didn't realize when they told me, how deeply this news affected me. It gradually seeped in and, by supper time, I was blaming myself for all the happenings. Without realizing it, I became convinced I was hurting my own family. When Phil was getting ready for work, he suddenly noticed how upset I was and told me to call my mother. I don't remember what I said to her but I know it alarmed her.

As Phil was leaving, I guess I started babbling. *This particular part is very hazy to me and I wonder if I were in some kind of shock. Hindsight rears its ugly head again.* I knew I was talking and couldn't stop even though I was not fully aware of what I was saying. Phil decided to stay home. He called mum again and told her he couldn't go in to work. She was glad he wasn't going to leave me. He took me down to the restaurant in town for a drink. The owners of the *Maple Manor* are friends of ours and Phil wanted me to tell Bernice all that had happened.

I knew she was busy running the business, and frankly, figured she'd think I was nuts. Thank God, she didn't. She listened and believed. She offered us shelter if we needed it and moral support which we freely acknowledged needing. I went home with a little of the tension relieved but my depression returned the minute I entered the house. It's amazing the effect the house has on everyone's feelings.

Jeff, Beth's boyfriend, was getting ready to leave when we got home. I believe I went right to bed, although my recollections of that day are extremely hazy. As Beth said goodnight to Jeff at the back door, both of them heard the sound of a shovel being dragged in the gravel down the road. I'm glad they didn't tell me about it until much later. Are they digging our graves?

Clara M. Miller

Wednesday—July 18, 1973

I was working up in my garden today when my brother, Martin, his wife Mikki and their daughter, Michele, pulled up in their car. They said they were just passing by and thought they'd drop in. Since they live on Grand Island, about 80 miles away, I detected my mother's fine hand in their visit and was suitably grateful. *I took them for a quick tour of the house, trying to laugh off the areas that frightened me. When I told Martin that I thought Vincent Price lived in the cellar, instead of laughing, he nodded solemnly as though he agreed with me. That kind of shook me.* We visited for a long time and Martin, who is a most sensible person, believed our story. He told me that Mikki was psychic and often scared him with her predictions. Phil tried, successfully, to talk them into staying the night. He probably thought he would have to stay home again if I didn't have someone else here. It gave me a good feeling to know they all cared even though I didn't consider all the concern necessary. *Denial? A false sense of security? Hubris? Who knows.*

Seeing Martin, I was reminded of his first visit to the house. Our front porch ceiling is unnaturally bulky looking and must have a large hollow space above it. Martin said at the time, "I think there are bodies buried in there!" Was he right?

We had another surprise visitor today. Bernice drove up with her waitress, Elaine, and wanted to take me to her house for the night. Even though I refused with thanks, she'll never know how good she made me feel. Elaine made me a little apprehensive though when she took our Ouija Board. We had seldom used it and then always as a game *with one memorable exception.* Perhaps I should include at this point the experience the kids had with the Ouija Board.

As I said, we considered the board a game and nothing more. However, when we first began having suspicions about the normality of the house, the kids decided to "ask the Ouija". I was not home. At the time, I kept a vigil light burning in front of a statue of Our Lady on the television set in the living room. The kids asked the Ouija Board what was going on and the planchette flew forcefully out from under their hands. After it did, the vigil light also became airborne and landed at their feet. Thankfully, the flame went out during its trip.

Beth had a doll at that time. It was the size of a two year old child and wore a two-year-old-child's clothes. Lately, it had seemed threatening to her. In an excess of high spirits, the kids hanged the doll. They swore it was looking at them. After cutting it down, it scared them so much, they hid it in a closet. It was subsequently given to Grace (our camping neighbor) for her daughter Susan. The first night the doll spent with them in their house back in Buffalo, their beds began to rock all over the room. They hadn't known the doll's history. Grace, frightened half out of her wits, got up and put the doll in their garbage can. She watched fearfully the next morning as a garbage man took the doll out of the can and put it in the truck. I sometimes wonder who he gave it to.

However, I still have no qualms about Ouija Boards. When our troubles started, we needed a target so we sprinkled it with Holy Water and kicked it until it was bent. The violent action served to relieve our feelings of helplessness, nothing more. Elaine insisted she would prove it was nothing but a "child's toy". I told her we didn't blame the board for anything but she kept insisting so I let her take it along when they left. Funny, though, I found out later she hadn't taken it home as she had said she would but had hidden it in the storage closet in the restaurant.

Thursday-July 19, 1973

Martin and Mikki had to leave early today. I think they're disappointed they didn't see a ghost. They sat up most of the night watching Dolly's nocturnal antics. She spent the better part of each night playing and was really a funny sight. I always thought that "Pepe le Pue's" antics were merely cartoon license but skunks really do jump stiff-legged like that! In spite of Martin and Mikki's disappointment, I'm glad nothing happened.

When Phil came home from work, he too was sorry that Martin and Mikki had to leave. I explained that Martin had a flying lesson and wasn't able to stay. Since Martin's discharge from the Air Force, he had been determined to learn to fly. He hadn't been allowed to receive pilot training in the service due to an ear injury. I remember one time Martin flew his rented plane down to the Olean airport to deliver Laura's birthday present. To say she was thrilled would be a gross understatement. *Laura, as middle child, always seemed to be lost in the shuffle. Her older brother and sister were high achievers. Her younger sister was more assertive as youngest often are. Laura vied for attention in sometimes dangerous ways although I didn't realize it at the time. She was diagnosed as a dyslexic but that was only half of her problem, something we didn't learn until much later.*

This morning I felt very restless and asked Phil if it was all right if I visited my girlfriend Shirley S, who recently moved to a house near Java Lake. This is not the same Shirley who used to visit our cabin with me but a former fellow-worker from the Iroquois Gas Company. The kids were anxious for an outing too so we set out on the 30 mile drive. *Shirley and her husband, Ray, had three children–two girls and a boy. We had been very close at one time and I really regret losing track of them just as I lost so much at this time.*

Shirley and Ray's house had, at one time, been a convent for nuns who ran a summer camp on the site, so, in addition to the house, they had playground equipment and two good sized cabins. The house itself is really fascinating. It's one of those places where you never know what will be around the next corner.

Since nuns had once lived there, it was well taken care of. I was intrigued by the nooks and crannies and I know I would really explore if I owned the place. It even had a butler's pantry, something I had never seen before. However, this was not the main reason I visited Shirley. I happened to remember that she had told me about playing host to a poltergeist in their former home. I thought I'd find out how they had handled the problem.

I told her what had been happening and that the tentative diagnosis had been poltergeists. Their poltergeist had become a family friend and they were able to talk to it so it didn't exactly parallel our case. Through all this talk I continue to feel as though I have been transported to the twilight zone. Talking to a poltergeist?

Shirley told me what she thought was causing our trouble. It seems that everyone has a theory. I should be used to it. She figures I am subconsciously causing the disturbances because I want to "get even" with Phil through the kids. I told her I found it hard to believe that I would harm the kids for any reason let alone vengeance. Vengeance, furthermore, is a rather harsh word. It is true that Phil and I have frequent differences of opinion. We are both extremely volatile people and, while I'm sure our arguments seem rather violent to the onlookers, in reality they are much less severe than they appear. I had to admit though, that our marriage was still rapidly deteriorating.

However, I did consider her theory and it did make some sense so I went away with a still larger sense of guilt. If I were, indeed, causing the trouble, whether consciously or subconsciously, I imagine Phil would be the motive. My head was spinning by the time I got home and I guess I was really depressed. Lately, I have been finding it harder and harder to keep my cool.

Sometimes I felt as though little pieces of me were dropping off and I was surprised that no one else seemed to notice. Life went on around me in some kind of fog and nothing seemed real to me anymore. I realized in some dim corner of my mind that it was summer and that I should be enjoying it. I knew it would probably be the last time I would have all the kids home and yet I couldn't really enjoy anything. Each day had become something to be endured; each night something to dread and each thought something to be mistrusted. Would anything ever get back to any semblance of normalcy? And, perhaps more important, would we survive until then?

Friday–July 20, 1973

I passed the day in a fog, as usual, and am really getting worried about my apathy. I am becoming incapable of completing a task. I have always loved to talk but I have become a compulsive talker–talking incessantly about the incidents we had experienced. I guess I hope by talking about them they will seem less extraordinary. Since it has become comparatively quiet,

I am now nervously waiting for the other shoe to drop. The oppressive atmosphere in the house has not changed and, indeed, in Mary's room is getting stronger every day. The constant rattling of the latch on the cellar door located in the bathroom, finally got on my nerves today and I shouted, "Shut up!" You know what? It did! *One good thing about having ghosts rattle a door right next to the toilet, no one in our house was ever constipated.*

When I weighed myself today, I was alarmed to see how much weight I was losing. I was down to 98 pounds. Since I'm five feet four and a half inches tall, that's too light.

Mum called today and, as usual, my gloom lifted a bit. She and dad were coming down Saturday. They had it all planned. Dad was going to stay at the house with the kids while I went back to Buffalo with mum for a few days. They thought I should get away from the house. Suddenly, I felt like I was seeing light at the end of a long, dark tunnel.

Sometimes I think the house is absorbing me. I can't seem to explain it to anyone but Beth. She is the only one who really seems to understand. Is she feeling the same way? I get the feeling she has the same thoughts about the house that I do. It frightens me to be always on the verge of tears, always exhausted, always drained and I am looking forward to the trip to Buffalo with profound relief. I know, deep down, that if I don't get away for a while, I will break down completely. Too much! Too much!

Saturday—July 21, 1973

It was good to see mum and dad again. After having lived so close to them for so many years, I had become used to talking any problem over with them. Since this nightmare started, it has been difficult to be unable to walk upstairs and find a sympathetic ear. However, I am beginning to get the feeling that Phil doesn't like the idea of my going to Buffalo. This morning, he acted annoyed and that's always a bad sign. I was surprised because I thought my need to get away was apparent. After all, he is able to find relief in going to work every day so he escapes the worst of the tension. I can't imagine why he would resent my getting at least this small chance for a break.

Sunday–July 22, 1973

Today is my sister, Cathie's birthday. I have forgotten birthdays, anniversaries and whatever else in this nightmare that had come upon us. I keep hoping it has ended but something tells me it is just beginning. I am afraid they are gaining in strength while we poor mortals are losing ours. Mum and I rode to Buffalo with Gordon so dad would have his car in case he needed it. Buffalo may be polluted but it looked mighty good to me today even through the smog. I wonder what kind of pollution they would say was present in our house. A more important question–if some of the haunting were my fault, would it follow me? I soon found out–it did no such thing.

Monday–July 23, 1973

I decided to call Charmaine and see if there were any way to meet the psychic who had told us about our envelopes. Maybe he would be able to help us–at least with advice. *At least he could clarify what he meant by my being the source of the power being used. I needed something to ease the guilt I felt.* She said she would arrange a meeting and, true to her word, said Maureen would pick me up on Tuesday and I could meet Wally. I hoped I wasn't grasping at straws again.

I called my girlfriend, Shirl, and she promised to come over and visit. We have been friends since our high school days at Mount Mercy Academy. *We both had to work our way through to pay the tuition so it gave us a close bond.* I looked forward to seeing her. I also wonder what she will think of all this. She has been an overnight guest many times since we moved to the country and I can't help wondering if she will continue her visits. For that reason alone, I am almost afraid to tell her what has been happening.

It was late when Shirl finally got to the house. Just as she was leaving her house, she discovered she had a flat tire. We had

a nice visit over a cup of tea. I'm not sure she believed all my story, still I think she did at least give me the benefit of the doubt.

Tuesday—July 24, 1973

Today is Martin's birthday. I don't remember whether I wished him a Happy Birthday when he visited us or not. Oh, well, we're having a combined party on the 28th so I'll tell him then. The day passed uneventfully. I don't have to worry about being haunted here, of catching a glimpse of someone or something out of the corner of my eye. I have lost the feeling of constant threat and the need to be constantly on guard. The sense of relief is profoundly welcome.

Maureen picked me up at 7:30 in the evening and I was amazed to find she had to drive me all the way to Lancaster to Wally's home. I hardly knew Maureen and was pleasantly surprised by her concern. On the way to the house she filled me in on Wally. He headed a study group to which she belonged. They had been connected with Rosary Hill College's Human Dimensions Institute but had since gone on their own to study psychic healing. Before I knew it, we pulled up in front of Wally's house.

Wally and his wife impressed me as such serene, happy people that I took to them immediately. Their house was lovely and the atmosphere very comfortable. I have become very sensitive to atmosphere. Again, I told the whole story while Wally sat in the darkening room and listened. I am beginning to feel like a tape recording. Wally's first question when I finished surprised me.

He asked me if I had suffered a sickness or injury which may have damaged my brain. I told him I had undergone an angiogram in 1968 and some of the dye had stuck in an artery in my neck. He correctly stated it was on the right side and told me I had slight brain damage on my right side. This was news to me but it made sense. If this is a sample of Wally's psychic diagnosis, it made a deep impression on me.

As for the ghosts, he thought we might have several types of haunting: poltergeists and, perhaps, spirits from more than one source. He tested me with his pendulum and told me I had psychic power and was probably providing some of the energy being expended in the house. This would account for my constant fatigue and accompanying weight loss. He also said I had nothing to do with the way this power was used. This helped my guilt feelings considerably. I left with the feeling I had new friends.

Wally promised that he would come down to the house as soon as possible and see what he could find out using his own power. Why does this still sound crazy to me? No matter how hard I try, I feel as though the whole thing is a put-on, a joke. But Wally was real and very sincere. I really didn't know how to thank him. I felt like such a babe in the woods in this field and I was very grateful for his patient explanations.

I was quite late getting home and, of course, had to tell mum a little of what had happened. Phil had called while I was gone and was greatly annoyed that I wasn't home. I don't want him to know about my visit with Wally until I can tell him the entire story in person. This whole affair has him pretty upset and I know he doesn't really believe in psychic powers, supernatural happenings and the whole Pandora's box which had suddenly opened up. I wonder if I do. All I can hope for is that he will at least try to understand. I would have to phrase my explanation carefully. I have the vague, uncomfortable feeling that I shouldn't have to.

Wednesday—July 25, 1973

I have been having a few qualms about leaving dad and the kids alone in that house although it seems like a fairly quiet time. I made a quick phone call this morning and was assured that things were okay. The only incidents they reported were the usual sounds of footsteps and knocking in Mary's room. That doesn't seem so awfully bad in view of the things that have been happening. I could now relax until the time came for Phil to pick me up.

Funny, it's been so quiet in the house. It sounds like the happenings run in cycles. There must be a pattern. I made plans to look for such a pattern when I returned home. Could it have something to do with the phases of the moon? *Do they expend their energy and have to renew it before resuming the harassment?* Or was it because I was gone that things were quiet? That was a possibility I didn't like to consider. I resolved to do more reading on this subject.

Shirl visited me again this evening and, while she isn't too willing to accept what happened, still I don't think we'll be seeing as much of her. She had a reaction which I've come to accept as normal. People don't believe in ghosts but they don't want to meet one!

Thursday—July 26, 1973

Phil came early this morning to pick me up. I guess I should be flattered that he wants me home so badly. If I hadn't had the break, though, I don't know what would have happened. All the way home we talked about my visit with Wally. Or rather, I talked. He didn't really approve of my seeing him. It's hard to make such things reasonable to someone who doesn't yet accept the fact that there is more in this world than is visible to us. Come to think of it, it is still very difficult for me to accept and I have been right in the middle of it.

At home things have held up pretty well. Thank God, the kids are so resilient. My dad is a quiet, thoughtful person. He manages to accept things as they are with very little resistance. His gentle presence has exerted a calming influence on the kids. The atmosphere doesn't seem as bad as it had before I left. Again, we wondered if the persecution were over. I guess it's true what they say about hope springing eternal.

Friday—July 27, 1973

Dick and Grace came down today with their two daughters. They are spending the weekend at their cabin so Susan and Darlene decided to spend the night with us. Since things had been quiet, I was not too worried. The weather is so hot! Breathing is difficult and almost uncomfortable. There didn't seem to be a breath of air moving. As always, the downstairs section of the house was comparatively cool while the upstairs felt like an oven.

The family is looking forward to the combined birthday party which is scheduled to take place tomorrow. Beth and I were going to bake the cake but, since it flopped, the less said about that the better. Keeping our fingers crossed, we called the bakery in Olean. Luckily, they were willing to make us a cake at the last minute with eleven names on it! *The girl who took the order was laughing when she hung up. I had to laugh with her. I don't suppose they get many orders for birthday cakes with eleven names!* We have so many birthdays in the summer we decided long ago to celebrate them all at once. The practice has grown so that not only our family birthdays are included but close friends as well. Everyone seems to get a kick out of having their names on our already overcrowded cake.

Phil and I had a hard time getting to sleep, it was so hot. I finally dropped off into a rather restless sleep and woke up suddenly exactly 10 minutes later by the clock. I was freezing. I touched Phil, who by this time was sound asleep. His skin felt as cold as ice. I had to check his breathing to make sure he was just sleeping. He always felt so warm but now he was so cold.

The hair on the back of my neck stood up and I knew my optimism of yesterday was premature. Just then, Mary came running upstairs and said that Gypsy was on the porch tearing the screen door apart. I had just heard Gyp walking around in the upper crawl space above our bedroom so I knew it couldn't be her. I ran downstairs and all four girls were standing by the front door in the kitchen, scared to death.

Quickly opening the door, I found that the screen had indeed been ripped but there was no animal in sight. The porch door was tightly closed so nothing could have gotten out that way. In addition, the porch was fully enclosed so nothing could have gotten in. I didn't make too much of it so I wouldn't frighten the girls further. I had a hard time getting back to sleep. I didn't wake Phil.

Saturday—July 28, 1973

THE PARTY! Everyone had a ball. I stopped counting after the first hour as more and more friends arrived. I remember talking to people. *Every time another carload of kids arrived, I remember laughingly telling Phil to open another package of hot dogs.* I remember laughing and watching everyone having a good time. Yet, with the exception of the knowledge that I had a good time, everything is kind of blurred. It's like a movie out of focus. I know I talked to people but have no recollection of what I said. I remember eating but don't know what I ate. A fog seems to be surrounding me at all times.

Shirl, mum and dad spent the night with us and my sister, Cathie, her husband, Mike and their kids, Gary and Karen, stayed with Gordon at his cabin down the road. *After visiting with us many times, Gordon had caught the "rural retreat fever" and bought a cabin from Donna and Ken just as we had years ago. It was situated on a hill and had a magnificent view. I wish he hadn't lost it years later.* Martin and Mikki decided they would go home with Michele.

When the house and grounds were echoing with laughter and good will it was hard to believe anything bad could ever happen here but I have a horrible feeling that soon I would have a reminder that bad things could happen. In fact, I feel that something is going to happen very soon. Am I psychic? *According to research books I have read since we left Hinsdale, the presence of so many people, especially when they were high-energy, added to the power saturating the area. Shot in the foot again!*

Mum offered to let Shirl sleep in Beth's bed but she chose Mike's instead. Funny, she says she doesn't believe in ghosts but I heard her say, "If I had my choice, I'd rather have boxes fall on me than something furry leap at me!"

The only incident that marred my day was a report that Susan had discovered a small, tear-shaped burn on her finger when she woke up this morning.

Sunday—July 29, 1973

It was such a beautiful day today we decided to eat outside again. We hate to waste the summer days which are always gone too soon. Mum and dad had to leave early to take Mike and Cathie home but Shirl stayed. We were fixing supper early so she wouldn't get too late a start for home. The route between here and Buffalo is ill-lighted at best and Shirl isn't used to the road.

The day was hot so Laura, Mary and Susan went swimming in the pond. Shirl and Phil were busy with the fire in the outdoor grill while I made the salad in the kitchen. A most idyllic scene! It was times like these that made me glad we moved to the country in spite of everything.

Just as I finished adding the dressing, Mary and Susan came into the kitchen with very puzzled expressions on their faces. They started telling me about a woman they had seen dancing on the other side of the pond. I don't think it occurred to them at first that the woman wasn't really there. *This is where I depart from the popular conception of "ghosts". They do not appear wispy....at least ours didn't. They looked as solid as everyone else so it's not easy to recognize one right away. Your conscious mind shies from such a conclusion anyway. It's only later the truth begins to sink in. Perhaps it's just as well. A little distance from the event might serve to blunt its effect.* They described her as having reddish hair, big blue eyes and buck teeth. They also agreed that her dress was made of "curtains" and that she spun around as she danced and disappeared into the tall grass. I haven't the faintest idea of how they could have seen all these details from a distance of about fifteen feet but they were both adamant.

As they told me about the woman, they became progressively more excited and it seemed to dawn on them that they had seen an apparition. We went out to tell Phil and he lost no time in running to the other side of the pond. Of course, there was no one in sight and no place anyone could hide. The girls walked around the pond with him, brave as long as he was at their side. They showed him exactly where she had been and how she had danced.

Watching them ape her eerie dance sent chills rippling up my spine. According to their version, it was a lazy type of, perhaps, interpretive dancing. They were both so sincere, and so obviously upset, there was no doubting that what they said was true. The only way the description varied was that to Mary the woman appeared to have "rabbit" teeth while Susan said her teeth were long and pointed and each tooth had a red line running down it. How could she see such a minute detail?

Strangely enough, although Laura had been in the pond with the girls, she had not seen the woman since she was facing the other way. The girls felt that Shirl did not believe them but I had a feeling she really did. The only other comment came from Mary and proved to be uncannily accurate. With the prescience of the young, she said, "I'll bet that lady hanged herself. Her eyes were bugging out of her head." Phil suggested I call Father Al. When I did, he said he'd be out as soon as possible.

Father arrived in the early evening with a friend, Father Dermit. I think Father Dermit was appalled at the happenings in the house and thought they should bless the house–again. Father Al assured him it had been blessed several times to no avail. Nevertheless, Father Dermit thought he should "throw some blessings around" just in case. He blessed the family and asked protection for us. At this point, Father Al had no explanation for the woman on the pond but assured us we wouldn't see her again. *Not to belabor the point, but by this time we tended to take Father's blanket assurances with a grain of salt.*

Tonight Craig and Randy stayed overnight with Mike and Darlene stayed with Beth so we had a full house again. I had gotten so used to extra kids in the house I hardly noticed. Since we moved in we had encouraged the kids to have their friends over, we lived so far from everyone. They had taken us up on it. Darlene slept in Mike's room and the boys on the living room floor.

Monday–July 30, 1973

We had a good night's sleep last night. This morning was something else. The three boys looked at each other as they came in for breakfast. Craig said to Mike, "I think you'd better tell her." Phrases to drive you out of your mind! They told me. It seemed that the boys spent the night listening to something being dragged around. At first they thought it was Darlene moving something in Mike's room but when they checked they found her sound asleep. They decided it must have come from the kitchen but each time they got up to check the sound stopped. Well, Phil and I had a good night's sleep anyway.

Wednesday—August 1, 1973

The heat is still unbearable, especially upstairs. Nights are beginning to be a real trial and last night was no exception. Since sleep eluded me, I was quick to hear a sound at the foot of the stairs. Afraid one of the kids was sick, I got up to check. As I reached the top of the stairs, I saw a young woman at the bottom, just passing by. Without thinking, I dismissed it as Beth. As I turned to go back to bed, I realized that it couldn't have been. In spite of the heat, a chill traced its finger down my back. The figure I saw was wearing a long, flannel nightgown trimmed with blue flowers and had long brown hair. Beth has short hair and she was wearing pink shortie pajamas. Quickly, I retraced my steps. The figure had been heading for Beth's room and that thought galvanized me. Racing down the steps and around the corner, my hair rose at the thought of what I might see. What did I see? Nothing. Beth was sleeping peacefully and so was Mike. No one else was in sight. More games.

Sunday—August 5, 1973

With growing optimism, I realized this morning that it's been several days since anything worth mentioning happened. Still, I'm afraid, this time, to hope it's over. Two of our birthday cake companions, Dan and Danae, dropped by today. Danae will be leaving for the Air Force pretty soon and we'll all miss her. Being her brother, Dan will miss her the most. While we stood talking in the yard Phil came out and asked me to talk him out of going to work. Thinking he was kidding, I just laughed. But, he wasn't kidding. He said he had a strong premonition that something was going to happen.

The second time he came out, he told me that Dolly was "stomping" all over upstairs and he thought there might be something wrong with her. I told him I thought Dolly was downstairs but he insisted. Humoring him, I checked under the couch and Dolly lay there, fast asleep. Phil said, "Then who's stomping around upstairs?" When he checked he found no one, not even one of the pets up there.

That settled it in his mind. Sure something was going to happen, he stayed home. As the evening progressed the atmosphere became more and more menacing and, perhaps, if Phil hadn't stayed home something dreadful would have happened. As it was, he spent the night sitting downstairs watching and waiting. Not a calming activity in our house, I assure you. I think he almost hoped something would happen to justify his vigil. However, I am grateful it didn't. Apparently, his presence paid off by keeping the house quiet and the atmosphere finally receded.

Earlier in the day we had received quite a blow. Some of our friends told us that Laura was accusing every male around of having molested her. The news really stunned us. Laura has a learning disability and had just been transferred back to her own school from special classes. Since she is dyslexic, she finds reading very difficult. This disability had led to many emotional problems. We were afraid she had endured some sort of setback. Could the house be affecting her?

The disconcerting thing about the whole thing was that when we questioned her we had the distinct feeling that it wasn't Laura who answered us. Her phrasing was different, strangely formal and old fashioned and there was an odd look in her eyes. In fact, she seemed impersonally amused by the whole thing. I couldn't understand it. Once more, I asked mum and dad to stop down so I could ask their advice.

Monday–August 6, 1973

Mary can no longer sleep in her room. It's lucky Phil works at night so Mary can sleep with me. The atmosphere in her room is unbelievable. There seems to be a vacuum in there. There is a strong, very discernible physical pressure on your ears and temples. It causes your ears to pop as though the atmosphere were rarified. The only comparison I can make is the feeling when your ears pop in an airplane. In addition, if anyone is outside the window, just a few feet away, it's as though they are worlds away and you can hardly hear them.

Even dad noticed that phenomenon the last time he was here and he doesn't claim to be sensitive to such things. Tonight Mary and I lay in bed listening to what sounded like furniture being moved around downstairs. When I went down to check, Beth said she was lying in bed listening to furniture being moved around upstairs in Mary's room. In addition, Mary's bed was creaking under someone's weight although the room was closed and empty. As least I think it was.

Tuesday–August 7, 1973

Mum and dad arrived this morning and we discussed Laura and what should be done. We all agreed that she should go home with them and spend a week or so. Perhaps the house is doing this. The idea seems incredible but I don't know what else would cause such an abrupt change in personality.

Wally came today too. Charmaine called this morning and told me that she and Maureen were bringing him down in Maureen's car. Wally has a bad leg and doesn't drive.

As usual, when they arrived the house really took a toll on Maureen's car. Wally's first words as he got out of the car were: "Something doesn't want me here." They told me that just before they left Buffalo, Maureen had several strange things happen to delay her departure. Then, as they turned onto our road, the exhaust system had fallen off her car. They wired it up and continued. When Maureen tried to pull the car up into the parking spot in our yard, the car refused to go into gear and they had to push it. Then they discovered it had developed a sudden gas leak. On hearing this, Maureen dissolved into tears. I don't know what it was with cars but the house sure has been hard on them.

I had told our friend, Betty S she could come up and meet Wally so I called her and let her know he had arrived. She said that Bob S, a reporter on the Olean newspaper, was visiting and she asked if he could come up with her if he promised not to print anything about the house.. Under those conditions we agreed. At the time I wasn't aware that the reporter was Betty's ex-husband. As usual, we had a house full of people so I'm afraid conditions must have been very trying for Wally.

After much concentration and meditation, he said he felt we were being bothered by a family who had lived here previously and didn't want us to have their house. He said he saw a mother, father, son and grandmother. He seemed to think that if we had been a quiet, elderly couple they wouldn't have bothered us. They did not approve of our noisy, "free-wheeling" family. *I have since come to realize that each psychic would have his own impression of our "visitors" and I believe whatever energy operates there determined from the psychic's own mind what to generate. There was only one psychic who didn't seem to fall under the spell of the house although even in his case I'm not positive.*

We hadn't told Wally where the different incidents had taken place and yet he knew that Mary's room was the worst in the house. Identifying cold spots throughout the house, he had broken out in a cold sweat in Mary's room. He also felt that there were more spirits in the kitchen than anywhere else. This caused some furtive looking around by the people in the kitchen. He said he thought they would leave whenever we REALLY wanted them to go.

Knowing that we have a subconscious, I thought that maybe we didn't really want them to go but were unaware of the fact. *Hindsight: Arrant nonsense!* I determined that we would all cultivate the desire to be rid of them. Actually, if our haunting were caused by a family who had loved the house and meant us no harm, I wouldn't have minded their staying. But this frightening atmosphere must stop!

Wally asked if we were getting any reaction from the animals. All I could say was that Jinx liked sleeping in whatever room seemed the most disturbed while Fluffy and Julie did their best to stay outside at night and the parakeets were making the strangest noises. I was wishing I had possessed the patience to teach the birds to talk as they might have been able to pick up something we couldn't hear and pass it on.

I told Wally that gradually and without realizing it, we began to use Fluffy as a barometer. If she slept in a room we knew it was "clear". I also related a rather strange incident involving Julie. One night she absolutely refused to come in and, since I don't want them wandering around *especially since Tyger's death,* I closed her in on the front porch. Again, the porch was fully enclosed and had a door that consistently jammed shut. We often had to kick it or pull it hard, it opened inward, to get it open. It also made a terrible noise of protest when it was opened. In the morning I got up to find Julie outside on the lawn and the door still closed. She was very frightened and wouldn't come in the house all day. I even had to feed her in the yard.

Betty and Bob were interested observers and Betty asked Wally questions about starting a psychic study group similar to his in our area. Wally, Maureen and Charmaine had a picnic at Charmaine's campsite while the men did their best to fix Maureen's car. They managed to repair it enough so that it would make it back to Buffalo and the trio left before it got dark.

Mum was sleeping in Beth's room again with Mary at her side on a cot. She had just gone to bed when I discovered another dollar was missing. We have been missing money at odd times for about a year and the total was mounting. It usually disappeared when no one was around to take it. I went in and told mum about it. With a smile, she informed me that she had just privately told the "grandmother" Wally had spoken about that if she were a grandmother she should be ashamed of herself. Now if she'd only listen.

I was not to find out until tomorrow that mum was visited by the "grandmother" shortly after I left the room. Mum was not yet asleep as she could hear us talking in the kitchen. She looked up toward the door and saw a woman standing at the side of Mary's cot. Since the figure was too tall for Mary and too short for me, she finally realized who it must be. As she watched, the "woman" disappeared. She was quite upset that she hadn't had the presence of mind to ask who she was and what she wanted. Since she saw only a silhouette, she could not give a good description. She thought the woman had something on her head–perhaps a veil-like covering. Since mum is acting so matter of face about the incident, Mary isn't too startled about having been so close to a ghost, or perhaps it hasn't hit her yet.

Wednesday–August 8, 1973

Since Wally agreed with us, most vehemently, that Laura should leave the house for a while, we decided she should go back to Buffalo with mum and dad. Wally had realized that Laura was affected by the house without my telling him. He asked me privately if she had undergone a drastic personality change just recently. When I confirmed his suspicions, he told me to get her out of the "damn house". He thought she may have picked up someone else's thoughts since he said he had sensed that a violent attack had taken place on a woman in the house many years ago.

In addition to this unnerving piece of news, Charmaine gave me more reason to worry. She told me that Laura had been swimming with her in her pond and Charmaine had told her not to swim out too far. Laura said, "It's okay; I know I'm going to die young and it doesn't matter because I've seen everything anyway." Charmaine said her eyes looked like a cat's eyes. She, too, felt she hadn't been talking to Laura–the same feeling we had. The description of her eyes as being like cats' eyes may be because Charmaine isn't too fond of cats. Nevertheless, since Charmaine hadn't known about the change in Laura, her report frightened me.

Mum and dad will be taking Laura to Buffalo tomorrow so, rather than have a big hassle, I told Mary she could go too. I'd just as soon both of them were out of the house until something is settled. Besides that, they're both helpful to mum. With her leg still in a cast, she needs all the help she can get. *Secretly, I know that to get away from the house until something is settled would probably entail moving to Buffalo.*

I explained to Laura what Wally had said and she promised to tell me if she gets any more weird ideas. *I get the distinct impression she's humoring me. Is it her?* It's going to be hard on her, suspecting every thought. At least she won't have to worry when she gets to Buffalo, Wally warned me that she is very psychic and, since she doesn't know how to control it, she is picking up vibrations from the house and misinterpreting them. This gets more complicated all the time! If I could only understand.

Mike has been out all day at his friends' houses, just visiting. He doesn't seem to like to stay home anymore and I don't blame him. This is his last summer at home and he feels he had to be in the house at dark in case anything happens. I'm not at all sure what he can do in any case. I went into his room tonight to pull the shade and felt eyes on me. I couldn't be sure of the feeling so I decided to test it. I brought Fluffy in and sat on the bed with her.

This normally complacent cat went crazy and scrambled out of my arms and out of the room as though she thought her life depended on it. I felt cold air moving and held my hands out over the bed. Cold air was rising from it! Cold air doesn't rise! I had this insane vision of my physics teacher saying "Warm air rises; cold air sinks." No sense, no sense at all.

I went into the living room and said to mum, "Why did you have to break your leg?" She knew what I meant right away and made everyone go into Mike's room to pray.

Guess who came home with Mike to spend the night: Randy—my spook chaser. He slept in Mike's bed and seemed to dispel the shadow in the room. Whatever he's got, I wish I could bottle it!

Friday–August 10, 1973

Every time a day goes by without an incident our hopes are renewed that "they" were gone. Just as we'd get some confidence, something new happened. It's as though they are laughing at all of us.

Today Phil called before coming home to see if I needed anything from the store and to ask if anything new had happened. Beth and I were in the kitchen, the only ones home. I had just reassured him that everything was fine when we heard a bang from upstairs. After I hung up, Beth ran upstairs to check. A large bottle of perfume which I always kept on my chest of drawers was lying on the floor on the opposite side of the room. Luckily, the bottle had a plastic coating and, so, did not break. Beth and I began to joke about their throwing things again.

When Phil came home a few minutes later he put two large bags full of bread and his lunch pail in the middle of the kitchen table and we walked out to check the garden. We inspected the vegetables. This is one of my most pleasant chores. I'll never get over the miracle of a garden. The soil here grows everything I plant and with very little effort on my part. *I do **not** have a green thumb!* I leave the upper rows to the deer who regularly come down to partake of my generosity. The only thing I have trouble growing is soy beans. Every time they attain more than a couple of inches in height, all the animals in the neighborhood come to the feast.

Gingerly, I told Phil about the perfume incident as we walked along the rows, joking about it. When we returned to the house, one bag of bread and his lunch pail were on the floor. The thermos inside the pail was smashed. Beth was standing by the front door, talking on the phone. When we asked her what had happened, she said they had just suddenly slid off the table as she was in the middle of her phone call. She acted as though this sort of thing were the norm, which by now, I guess it is. I wish they'd quit breaking things.

Sunday—August 12, 1973

Darlene and Susan stopped down to visit this evening. I sat down at the kitchen table with them. Beth and Jeff joined us. We were laughing and joking. I was telling them of my visit to meet my in-laws before Phil and I were married and how awkward I felt. I, the typical city-slicker, couldn't seem to connect with Phil's Virginia hill-bred relatives. The feeling in the house was quite light and normal.

Phil had left for work a short time before and I was startled when the phone rang and it was him. He asked if anything were wrong at the house. He said that, as he was driving to work, he suddenly broke out in a cold sweat and shook all the rest of the drive in. I was able to reassure him and he seemed relieved. He did advise me to be careful, though. I kind of laughed his advice off. I felt no threat in the house.

I hung up the phone and sat down at the table again. We resumed our light-hearted conversation. Beth and I had put the parakeets out on the porch for an airing early in the day and though it was after dark now, the temperature was still quite high. We knew that was not what caused them to go crazy in their cages. Suddenly, they began flying around like maniacs. We must have all jumped a foot at the resultant sounds. The only thing we could think of that would cause them to act like that was a sudden wind although none was apparent.

Beth and I immediately went out and brought the birds in. Since I was in charge of Mary's bird, Jingles, while she was in Buffalo, I hung him up on his hook in the living room. Mary was no longer able to keep him in her own room. Beth, in the meantime, had spilled some of Pixie's water and so, was delayed in getting back to the kitchen. I had only just sat down when Beth screamed. I knew that scream and began to run for her room. Jeff and the girls were paralyzed. Such is the effect of the terror generated by that particular scream. I had to dodge all three of them to get to Beth.

When I reached her room, Beth was huddled on her bed, her face buried in her hands, crying. She kept screaming, "She's in the window. Don't look!" I ran over and slammed the window shut and then pulled the shade down. My spine was crawling as I did so, although I could see nothing. Beth explained, between sobs, how she had climbed onto her desk chair to hang Pixie up when she sensed someone behind her. When she looked, she saw the face of a woman with long dark hair in the window beckoning to her. She could not be sure whether she was inside or outside.

Seeing her condition, I got very angry. I asked Jeff to go with me and we went outside to search. I was shaking, partly from anger and partly because, frankly, I was frightened. Jeff was even more afraid than I was. I challenged the "woman" to show herself to me instead of bothering the kids. Jeff kept muttering, "Don't call her. Just be quiet!" I didn't expect to find anything but the activity kept me from getting even more upset. I also hoped that some action, no matter how ineffectual, would serve to reassure Beth.

When we returned to the house Beth was trying to get seeds for the bird and succeeding only in spilling them all over the floor. She was shaking badly and still crying. The other two girls were practically hysterical. We had three very pale kids for a while. Come to think of it, I don't know what color Jeff and I were.

When Beth calmed down she tried to describe the woman. She said her hair was filthy (or wet) and all she really saw was her hair, big dark eyes and the beckoning hand. Shaking and terrified, Beth described the woman's complexion as pasty white, almost dead looking. When I entered the room I felt as though a fist had hit me in the stomach. It was very hard to go through the door and even harder to walk to the window and pull down the shade. For a long while, just as Mary would not swim in the pond, Beth would not enter a room after dark unless the window was closed and the shade pulled down.

Monday—August 13, 1973

I have been hearing such wild rumors as to the strange goings-on up at the house that when Bob, the reporter for the Olean newspaper called and asked if he could do a story I decided to talk it over with Phil. One of the crazy stories was that a picture on our wall was bleeding! We didn't have enough goofy things happening but people had to make up their own versions. Maybe it would be better if they had the true story even though it wasn't as spectacular.

After much consideration, we decided to let him do a story as long as he didn't use our name or give the location of the house. We figured those who were involved would know who it was and it was no one else's business. We pictured one of those filler-type articles, buried on the back page. We also hoped that someone might be able to tell us the past history of the house so we'd be able to pinpoint the trouble and, hopefully, do something about it. This was one way of reaching people who might know. We were in for a big surprise!

Tuesday–August 14, 1973

Bob came today to interview us for the story. He took some pictures of the house but, since it looks like a million other houses, nothing remarkable about it at all, we figured no one would recognize it. We gave him as complete a story as we could and hoped he would get it straight. At least he didn't make fun of us.

Thursday–August 16, 1973

Last night, I decided to sleep in Mary's room. Knowing it was foolish, I felt I had to know myself what was going on in there. What I hoped to find, I don't know. The temperature continued to be oppressively hot and nowhere more so than in Mary's tiny, airless bedroom. Having been closed up for some time, no fresh air had a chance to circulate. At my usual time, I climbed into her bed, clutching Fluffy tightly to my chest as a makeshift barometer. To my relief, she settled right down in the bed with me and appeared to go to sleep.

Whether I dropped off or not, I'm not sure. All I know is that suddenly I became aware of a precipitous drop in temperature. At the same time, I saw Fluffy leap off the bed and leave the room at a fast trot. The hair on the back of my neck began to prickle. Sitting up in bed, I looked out the door and directly into Jinx's unblinking eyes. The unnerving stare could only be described as malevolent. Was this my beloved Jinx? Remembering a warning from Wally, I decided to remind Jinx who I was. Quietly, while inching from the bed, I began talking to her in a soothing voice. At first, she didn't respond and I began to think she'd try to prevent my leaving the room. Gradually, though, she began to change in front of my eyes. The rigid at-attention stance relaxed and softened. Incredibly, the evil stare became her usual inquiring gaze and, slowly, she began to groom herself. By this time, I had reached the door. Quickly scanning the room, I closed the door and determined that, unless something changed dramatically, this room would not house another sleeper.

Friday—August 17, 1973

The story of the house was in the paper today. They gave it a front page spread! In fact, it took up half the front page and most of page three. In the center of the front page was a large picture of the house itself. On page three was a picture taken from Beth's window and a shot of the house taken from across the pond. Beth was upset because he took the picture in her room before she had a chance to rehang her just-washed curtains.

I had to go to Olean so I decided to stop in and see the girl I used to work with. I showed Rita the paper. Debbie, who had been a student when I worked at BOCES (Board of Cooperative Educational Services), was working in the Data Processing Department and she, too, looked at the article. I told them I hoped the publicity would bring some information that would help us but I was also a little worried about the effects such a big write-up would have.

My worst fears were realized. No sooner had I arrived home and begun to fix supper than the first car came–all the way from Salamanca. I don't really know what they came to see. We had a steady parade up our road and into our driveway until long after dark. In fact, one family drove up as we were eating, opened the door, walked in and sat down at our table with us announcing "We want to see a ghost!" We had never seen them before! I leave Phil's reaction to your imagination.

Imagine how many we would have had come if the location of the house had been given in the paper. Actually, all the secrecy had accomplished was slowing them down and testing their ingenuity. I'll never underestimate the resourcefulness of the "interested observer" again. I think this may be part of the breed that congregates around accidents and fires.

Saturday–August 18, 1973

Unbelievable! The cars just keep coming. Since we're at the end of a dead-end road, they either turn around in our yard or back all the way up the road. Debbie called today and asked if she could bring her boyfriend, Paul K, up to see the house. He thought he was psychic (doesn't everyone?) and wanted to find out for sure. How he'd find out up here is something I don't know. Phil refused to give his permission. He didn't know either of them so I couldn't blame him. He was really furious by now and, although he told me I could give the okay for the article, he was now blaming the whole thing on me. We tried keeping track of the number of cars coming down the road but soon gave that up. It was just too much trouble.

Gordon was staying the weekend at his cabin so I finally called him and he came down to help. He sat on a chair in our driveway with a .22 rifle. It wasn't loaded but no one knew that. Some of them turned when they saw him and other screamed obscenities at us. I never knew people could behave like that. We couldn't figure out what they wanted from us. They would drive up from a city one hundred miles away and yell at us, "We don't believe in ghosts!" No one has ever been able to explain to me–if that were the case why did they come?

In the evening, who should show up but Debbie and Paul K with Debbie's brother. I'm still not sure how they conned their way past Phil, who by now had been reduced to a state bordering on insanity. I have since learned to respect Paul's powers of persuasion.

Paul was very interested in the supernatural but it really frightened him. He and Phil took a walk outside and he held on to Phil's shirt the whole time. It was still spooky out at night so I guess I didn't blame him.

Clara M. Miller

Sunday-August 19, 1973

Today Beth and I went to Buffalo to pick up Laura and Mary. I have many misgivings about bringing them home with all the traffic our road has suddenly acquired. Actually, it isn't so much the quantity as the quality.

When we got back Phil was beside himself. He had chased 130 cars! Gordon was with him all day trying to help. In addition we were getting all sorts of offers of "help". These ranged from someone offering to take the spirits into his own body and then exorcizing them to a friend assuring us that some enemy was trying to get us to move. We appreciated all sincere offers of help, but, of course, many made fun of us. One of the secretaries from school was parked up the road watching us and, of all things, a State Trooper from town had his car parked so his family could climb on the roof and watch the house. These were the same people who were calling **us** crazy!

Monday-August 20, 1973

Still no let up. It isn't so bad during the day when people are at work but after supper the procession starts in earnest. Phil leaves for work at 9 o'clock and Mike and I are usually up until 2 or 3 in the morning chasing people. Sometimes they start screaming and shouting at us. Mike feels responsible for us when his father isn't home and it's just too much for a 17 year old. I can see him changing as I watch.

There was another, smaller article in the paper about the house. In it, Bob talked about the reaction he had received to his first article. From the way he wrote, there are more believers than non-believers, or at least they are more communicative. We are being roundly condemned by many from other rumors I heard. I wish Bob hadn't printed the second article. We have suffered quite enough after the first.

Tuesday—August 21, 1973

Things continue pretty much the same. Every day we chase cars far into the night. We are always afraid some of the people might have guns. Guns are common in the country and we don't want to have that kind of trouble. We wound up having to call the State Troopers for help and they said they would have the town set up a roadblock. We have been using our car to block the end of the driveway, forcing people to back down the road but even that hasn't discouraged them. We have no right to block the road, even though we are the only ones living on it.

An interesting sidelight developed, though, in our talk with the State Trooper who visited us. As he stood on our porch, he confided that he grew up only a couple of miles from the house so he was quite familiar with the area. As always, when we had a "local" cornered, we mentioned the "boy" and he looked shocked. The description closely fitted his brother who died about 20 years ago. The boy had been just the right age, 16, and the clothes he always wore fit the appearance of our "friend". His brother had been killed in an accident involving a buzz saw. I think the trooper kept a close watch on the road as he left.

Wednesday—August 22, 1973

One amusing facet of this whole debacle is that we are seeing a new and entirely unsuspected aspect of Father Al. Since first meeting him, I had regarded him as shy and rather serious. To the delight of the whole family, we were wrong. Several times since the story appeared in the paper he has come up to help chase away trespassers. Attached to the roof of his car was a portable rotating light that he usually used for campus security. Now he used it for our "security". The sight of the flashing light was enough to send many of the onlookers fleeing, at least the younger ones.

Some of our "visitors" were enterprising enough to drive up the camp roads and then double back across the hills to our house on foot. Father followed many of them up the road and they promptly left, believing they were being chased by the police.

The girls often accompanied him and they had the time of their lives. Maybe it gave them a badly needed sense of power. Certainly, it raised our spirits and provided a few badly needed laughs. Lately we seem to have lost control of our lives. At least in this small matter, we have the upper hand. And Father is having a grand time acting as our protector. The sight of his impish grin when yet another carload of teenagers reacted to the light made my day.

Sunday—August 26, 1973

A Mrs. G called today from Olean, with a familiar petition. Ordinarily, I brushed aside such calls as I can't possibly talk to everyone who is interested. However, Mrs. G at least deserved to be heard out due to the persistence with which she tracked down our phone number. She had read in the paper that our new station wagon had caused us a great deal of trouble. Her daughter-in-law worked in the dealership that had sold us our car and Mrs. G remembered her speaking of a family that had experienced constant trouble with their new car. She called her daughter-in-law who requested our name from the service manager. From such threads!

I told her she could stop in after she said she had been looking for some proof of life after death. Besides, such persistence in tracking us down deserved some reward. She showed up this evening with her son, daughter-in-law and a friend who, like everyone else I've met lately, claims to be a psychic. This friend, at any rate, claimed to see a Revolutionary War soldier marching through our living room! I'm sure he was very sincere so I won't comment on his allegation. He then gave us specially blessed candles and told us we would have no further trouble if we burned them in the most disturbed room in the house. We took the candles and thanked him for his concern. After hearing the story of our house, our company left.

As everyone reading this knows, the most disturbed room in the house would have to be Mary's. Again, willing to try anything, we went to light the candles. Mary's room was cold, as it often was, even in the summer heat. I put the candles in dishes and lit them. Just as the flame caught, a stuffed animal of Mary's that was hanging from the ceiling of that windless room, swung and hit me in the back of the head–hard! There was no normal explanation. It crossed a distance of at least three feet.

After the candles had burned down we again closed Mary's door. We had considerable trouble getting to sleep tonight because I kept having to check the annoying scratching noises under Mary's bed. There was nothing under the bed or anywhere else in the small room to account for the noises. Nor was there anything to explain the fact that, in the morning, her collection of birds' nests, stored under the bed, had been torn apart and scattered all over her room. I guess a collection of birds' nests doesn't seem so awfully important but it was important to Mary. She had collected those things since we bought the cabin and they meant a great deal to her. With a sigh, I reaffirmed my determination that no one enter that room unless it was an absolute necessity.

As we were getting ready for bed, Beth called me to check her room. There was a very strong smell in the room like the smell of carrion. The same smell you encounter when you come upon a long dead animal in the woods. We talked about it for a few minutes and the smell gradually faded.

I no sooner sighed with relief, when Laura called me. Her upstairs room smelled exactly the same way Beth's had. The odor was nauseating. After about 15 minutes the smell gradually disappeared. However, between my trips to check on the scratching under Mary's bed I had to check Laura. She kept feeling someone touching her shoulder. Also, her shoulder strap purse, hanging from a hook over her bed kept swinging, although there was no reason it should. Crazy! Is this all supposed to mean something? *For a long time, we drove ourselves crazy trying to find messages in everything that happened. We finally conceded that they weren't trying to send us a message. They just wanted to frighten us.*

Several people have suggested that we try "automatic writing". Ever hopeful, I left a pencil and paper on the kitchen table but apparently our "guests" are not interested in written communication. As I laid the writing implements out, I couldn't believe I was doing it. Was I beginning to believe all this stuff?

Monday–August 27, 1973

I made another interesting discovery last night. Paul has been coming up with another of his friends, a boy named Tim C. They would arrive after we went to bed and leave before we woke. As long as they stayed in Tim's car parked in our yard, conditions weren't as bad in the house.

Last night, as they were "patrolling" the grounds, they swore they saw Phil standing beside the spring house and, frankly, expected him to get after them. When I saw Phil, I asked him what he had been doing at that exact time (he was at work). He said it was during his lunch hour and he had taken a nap. The only thing was that during his nap he kept hearing me calling him. He must have really been worried about us. I tried putting myself in his place and realized how upset that would have made me–having to leave my family every night when I thought they were in danger. He had talked a lot recently about getting a job closer to home so he wouldn't have to leave us in the evening. It would mean giving up a good job and very good pay. We can't afford it.

Earlier today, I had been startled when all the alarm clocks in the house went off at once. It was one o'clock in the afternoon and my clock was always set to go off at 7 a.m. The setting hadn't been changed but the alarm buzzed away. In addition, one of the clocks that went off, the one in Mary's room, hadn't worked for months. Unfortunately, after I turned its alarm off it returned to its non-working condition.

All day long the electric stove kept turning on and off. I was getting worried for fear it would turn on at night and start a fire.

This evening when we were sitting in the living room the back door suddenly opened and we were treated to a blast of Arctic air. It was so strong a wind that all the curtains blew. I checked. The temperature outside was a balmy 80 degrees and there was no wind!

Tuesday—August 28, 1973

Well, it happened. I heard Laura getting up to go to the bathroom about three o'clock this morning. For a couple of months now, the best I could manage was a semi-sleep so I woke easily and often every night. Laura passed my door and I heard her gasp. I got right up not knowing what to expect. At first, with the red glow coming up the stairs I thought the house was on fire. The burners of the stove were all on and must have been on for some time as they were almost white hot. Thank God nothing fell on them!

Wednesday—August 29, 1973

Complaints from Beth become more frequent every day. I wonder if her room being directly under Mary's has anything to do with the disturbances she's experiencing. Last night she again felt someone sitting on the foot of her bed. When my mother sleeps there on her visits, she always complains about the same thing. Since we moved in, even before we knew the house was troubled, mum had said someone was sitting at her feet.

Beth also spoke of voices outside her window although she said they were too indistinct to make out individual words. I wonder if this could be her imagination. I certainly couldn't blame her for imagining things.

The last time I talked with mum she told me she thought she had a run-in with Beth's furry creature some time ago. She had dismissed the incident at the time, thinking it was a dream. Now she wasn't so sure. She had stayed overnight when Beth had her arm in a cast and insisted on sleeping on the couch. During the night, she woke to find something pulling her covers off. Looking down, expecting to see one of our pets, she was surprised to find a creature resembling a round fur ball. At first she was frightened but then she got mad and shouted, "Go back to Hell where you belong!" The tugging stopped immediately.

I wonder if this is the answer. Should we have gotten angry? Different people have suggested asking questions. It's okay in theory but any experience we have had is totally unexpected. I defy anyone to keep their cool when startled. It's a sad fact but true that you very seldom expect to encounter psychic phenomena.

Father Al came to visit today and said Mass on our kitchen table. Afterwards, he said a simple exorcism and carried the host around the house and grounds. Even though I am a lifelong Catholic, the ceremony gave me chills. There was a power there that couldn't be denied. Now, if only the power can counteract whatever other power we have as a constant resident here.

Actually, Father comes as often as he can and always cheers us up. Since he teaches at St. Bonaventure University, I'm sure it's not always easy for him to get away. I have a feeling, though, that some of the confidence he instills is done by conning us. *A placebo effect?* I don't mean that in a bad way. I think he believes that if he convinces us that he has taken a ghost home with him (which he frequently says) we won't be disturbed by it anymore. I haven't said anything because if it works for the kids I don't mind. Personally, since we still have ghosts I don't think the "con" works.

Thursday–August 30, 1973

Beth's room is "jumping" today. We have developed many "codes" when we mean a room is "disturbed"–"jumping" is one of them. I don't know how to describe a hostile atmosphere to someone who has never experienced one but I'll try. Suddenly, for no apparent reason, you're restless; sometimes you feel as though something is watching and waiting; or you get the vague feeling there is something you're forgetting to do; an uneasy feeling of fear, depression or apprehension. Have you ever been present at a friend's house when there was obvious tension in the air and you feel you've interrupted a quarrel? That uneasy, squirmy feeling is much the same. I guess uncomfortable is the word that best describes the feeling. All this really means nothing, I suppose, since you must experience it to know what I mean.

Mary took, her statue/nightlight back and put it in her room. Beth has a small 7 watt nightlight in her lamp. Today it burned out so we went up to Mary's closed room and found her nightlight flung on the floor. The room has been closed for some time and no one has been in it. No one wants to go near it. The base of the statue was smashed and Mary is very upset about it. She's also unhappy since one of her purses, the one she uses every day, disappeared. After much searching it was found **in her room**, a room she wouldn't enter even if she had a bodyguard with her! How much power is required to teleport a purse?

Beth is getting more upset daily about the voices she hears outside her window. Somehow, I'm going to have to find a way to listen in.

Friday—August 31, 1973

Today I was cleaning in my room and passed by Mary's door. Just as I did, there was an extremely loud knock on her door coming from inside her room. After I caught my breath, I opened the door to be greeted by nothing but the usual frigid air.

Paul and Tim have been reporting strange shapes in the fog and seemingly disembodied eyes. I saw the eyes last night myself near the pond so I knew what they meant. The boys set up a lantern near where they had seen the eyes but they didn't disappear. Any animal would run from a burning lantern but the eyes remained. Some animals are drawn to light it's true but these eyes stayed, unblinkingly, in one place until you approached them. Just as had happened in the incident with Jinx, the eyes would abruptly disappear only to reappear when the boys were at a distance. The area involved was on open ground with no grass. The boys were also frightened of the fog since it seemed to assume shapes and move in some kind of pattern. They really seemed to be having trouble outside.

Another disturbing report reached out ears today. From the stories I've heard, there were four or five people traveling on a road about a mile from the house. It was the middle of the night. Suddenly, a boy of about sixteen ran right in front of them. All the witnesses said the car hit him, knocked him down and then ran over him. When they stopped, they saw the boy get up and run into the fields. The driver of the car called the police and the fire department when they were unable to find him themselves. Both organizations searched the fields in the area but found on one. I have no explanation and can only report it third hand but, of course, many people think it's our "boy" and are very vocal about it. The mysteries keep piling up and the authorities refuse to make a statement. I don't blame them. They must be as confused as we are.

Saturday-September 1, 1973

Today, Charmaine's mother, Helen T, came down to report seeing an apparition. If you remember, their camp is directly above us but quite a distance away through open fields. She had been badly frightened. She told me she was in their camping trailer when she looked out the window and saw the upper half of a woman dressed in a sheer, gauzy dress. The woman was swaying to and fro in the semblance of a dance. Helen yelped and Charmaine reached for their .22. By the time she got outside, the woman was gone although a disturbed atmosphere remained. Helen promptly named the woman "Agatha." She said if she saw her again, she'd sell the campsite.

Martin, Mikki and Michele, mum and dad and Gordon, Cathie, Mike, Gary and Karen all come down today for an early Labor Day picnic. Cathie and her family are going to stay overnight with Gordon at his cabin down the road and mum and dad are staying with us. Martin and his family planned on leaving after dinner.

While we were getting dinner ready, Mikki suddenly gasped. She had looked up as she passed our stairway and had seen a woman's face. It was fuzzy and indistinct but it startled her. She was quite shaken for a while. Mikki is Japanese and, Martin says, very psychic. No wonder she was able to see the woman. I wonder which one it was.

When everyone left, we settled down and Beth spent the night in Mike's room. The house slept–or did it?

Sunday–September 2, 1973

I found out this morning that Beth didn't sleep well last night. She kept hearing noises coming from the crawl space over her head. Trying to explain, she said it sounded like someone moving something from one place to another. In fact, she even thought she heard grunts. Since I was determined to ignore noises, I told her to forget it. I was convinced the noises were intended to unnerve us (which they did). No one checked the crawl space.

Monday–LABOR DAY–September 3, 1973

Again–complaints from Beth about noises in the crawl space and again–we ignored her. Paul and Debbie stopped by to have a picnic dinner with us. The rest of our company had left so they wouldn't be caught in the heavy holiday traffic.

As we sat down to dinner, I began to get a strange, "prickly" feeling that something was wrong. Jeff dropped by and joined the party. As the time passed, the odd feeling intensified. Paul felt it too, although neither of us said anything. We exchanged glances that proved to me that our feelings were similar. He was becoming progressively more psychic and could often predict things with astonishing accuracy.

Without any warning, Paul stood up and announced his intention of walking past the pond over to the tree line at the end of our property. I felt such a sense of panic when he said it, I almost shouted at him. I told him I wouldn't let him go. Debbie agreed with me and we all went inside. Sitting on the couch, we began visiting when we heard loud footsteps coming from Mary's room. Debbie made some remark about noisy people until I told her that no one was upstairs. It was the first time she had heard any of our "noises". Paul rushed upstairs, opened the door and encountered only the usual icy air. Debbie began to get very nervous and it wasn't long before they went home. Quiet reigned–for a while.

It was getting near time for Phil to leave for work when he suddenly announced he wasn't going in. He knew he would lose the holiday pay if he didn't go so I knew something was really wrong. I, of course, tried to talk him into going. We just couldn't afford to lose the pay. He said he felt something coming from the tree line. I refused to admit feeling it and assured him that we could handle anything that happened (famous last words). He finally decided to check the grounds and then see how he felt.

He started toward the pond. I was about eight feet behind him, giving him all the reasons he should go to work, when I thought I saw someone dart around the house toward the porch. I stopped and looked but could see nothing. Phil obviously hadn't seen it. I ran to catch up with him, getting my feet wet in the pond runoff. We circled the pond and encountered several curiously cold spots. The coldest was at the far end of the pond where the girls had seen the woman dancing. We could see our breath. Don't forget–it was a hot September night.

Phil still wanted to walk to the tree line. Again, the ominous feeling! Something told me to avoid the tree line. I persuaded him to go back to the house. As we reached the end of the pond and started toward the house. I looked up to see a girl in Beth's window. She had strawberry blonde hair and was wearing what looked like a pink dust cap. I thought she was sitting on Beth's bed but a check the next day showed she must have been kneeling in front of Beth's dresser.

I just started to call Phil's attention to the window when Beth and Jeff came from the front of the house and asked if we had just crossed the front lawn. They had been sitting on the front porch when a figure dressed in white crossed in front of them (the same one I saw?). it was now dusk and the light was beginning to fail. Phil told me to go up to the neighbor's cabin and get a better flashlight than the one we had.

Mary, Laura and I got into the car and made the trip up the hill, returning minutes later with the light, a heavy duty lantern-type flashlight. After parking the car, Laura and I joined Phil in the driveway. He had found a path in the tall grass and was sure we had a trespasser. I told him there were all kinds of paths in the grass made by animals, both wild and our own pets. However, he was looking for a "natural" explanation. Mary, in the meantime, had joined Beth in the yard. They were watching Jeff sweeping the pond with the headlight of his motorcycle. Phil was patiently explaining his trespasser theory to me when Mary screamed.

It sounded exactly like Beth's scream so I knew what the cause must be. We ran to the yard. By the time we reached them, Jeff was frantically honking the horn on his cycle and Beth was trying to calm Mary. They explained that Mary had seen a woman looking at her from her own window. Beth had looked up just as the curtain was being dropped. We ran for the house.

It had been light when Phil and I left the house so no lamps had been turned on as yet. When we entered the kitchen we realized that all the lights upstairs were blazing. We hadn't even been upstairs for hours. Our hair stood on end. Phil told me to keep Mary and Laura in the kitchen while he searched (I guess he still had trespassers in his mind). There was nothing upstairs so he came down and went in to check the cellar. The door, which was always kept bolted, was standing wide open. Mary was still crying hysterically. I didn't know what to do. I felt restless and unable to stand still but, perversely, my feet didn't want to move.

In the middle of all this confusion, Mike called. He was at a friend's party and wanted permission to stay later. I told him we needed him home right away but to be very careful driving. A little while later, he and Randy drove up. For a while we had mass confusion. Randy's spook-chasing power didn't work this time. Beth and Jeff saw a man standing on the front lawn at the corner of the house. Phil ran out there only to have someone scream that there was something or someone in the yard. It got so I couldn't look at the windows because every time I did I got the impression of something passing by.

Mike and Randy got in the station wagon and drove down the road to make sure we had no trespassers and satisfy Phil. As they drove, they looked at the back seat and were startled to see a depression in the cushion as though someone were sitting there. What really made it frightening was that every time they hit a bump, the depression changed accordingly. Needless to say, they came right home.

At this point, Beth decided to turn on the TV to have some normal noise in the house. She walked to the living room and let out a scream that would curl your hair. I ran in and she said a girl was sitting on the foot of her bed. She described the same girl I had seen earlier in the window, a girl I had told no one about as yet.

I went in to check. There was a depression on the bed, as though someone had just gotten up. I felt it. The spot was warm! Were ghosts warm? There was absolutely no way anyone could have gotten out of that room without being seen!

Just then Phil called. He had gone upstairs again and found all the lights out this time. On his way down the stairs, he opened the crawl space and nearly fainted. Our chimney, which had been neatly mortared, was taken apart, brick by brick, and carefully stacked against the other wall. So, Beth **had** heard something. When Beth saw the chimney, or what was left of it, she began to cry.

I left her in Jeff's care while I went to call Father Al. He promised to come right over so we gathered in the living room to wait for him. I felt as though we were under siege. No one looked out the windows and no one moved from the room. We were terrified at what we might see. Frankly, I'm afraid no one's color was normal. When Father arrived, Phil told him all that had happened, finding it hard to keep the incredulity out of his voice. It's really awful when you can't believe what's happening even while it's happening.

They checked the house over together then they split up and investigated further. Father was questioning me in the kitchen when Phil called me from the yard. He had Father's five cell flashlight and was pointing it toward the pond. He asked what I saw in the beam. I looked and was amazed to see what appeared to be a young girl wearing a long, sheer gown walking along the path *on the other side of the pond, near where the dancing figure had been seen.* I told him and he asked, "What color is the gown?" As I looked, it changed from white to purple and back again.

When we called to Father, he offered to hold the light while Phil went down to the pond. As much psychic investigating as Father does, he has yet to have a truly personal psychic experience. Perhaps his subconscious wouldn't allow him to. Phil ran across the yard, calling the apparition every name he could think of but, naturally, couldn't find her. We returned to the house and, when everyone calmed down, I insisted they all go to bed. Phil and Father kept watch until early morning so we could sleep.

Hereafter, Labor Day 1973 was referred to as "the day all Hell broke loose!"

Tuesday—September 4, 1973

Phil was sick all day today. I guess it must have hit him suddenly that all we have been saying is true.

This morning I couldn't find my purse. Finally, it was located behind the bathroom door on the scale. Four dollars was missing. Father had warned us that the money disappearing could be a way of splitting the family up. Each of us would blame the other for stealing. I know the purse was in its accustomed place in my room when I went to bed last night.

We have been trying to make some sense out of yesterday's happenings but so far—no luck. Going over the "spirits" we had seen or which had been seen by others we came up with the following: the old farmer (the "black man"), the young boy, the redhead (could the woman by the pond, "Agatha" and the woman in the window be the same one?), the strawberry blonde (Beth, Mary and I had all seen her), plus the assorted figures of no definite description which we had all seen flitting around the property.

Who belonged to the perfume we occasionally smelled in Mary's room? Who smoked the pipe whose aroma was noticed in the living room near Beth's bedroom door and in the bathroom by the cellar door? And who belongs to the threatening voices Beth hears nightly outside her window? I began to take those voices more seriously. Sometimes I wish I were Sherlock Holmes!

I read somewhere about this time that many years ago an itinerant preacher and his spinster sister used to travel in the area. He hated women and, though he claimed hospitality from his "congregants", carried his own sheets so he wouldn't sleep on any sheets a woman was liable to have slept on. I wonder–are the pair back?

This afternoon, Gary D, a friend of ours from Buffalo, came to give us a copy of a book of his poetry as a gift. It had just been published and we were really pleased to get it. *Gary's family was the one that owned property down the road from our cabin near Cuba. He attended State University College at Buffalo when I worked there.* It was a relief to talk to someone who knew nothing about the house so we could hold a normal conversation for a change. Before he left, Gary took the boat out on the pond. After rowing it around for a while, he carefully pulled it right up on the shore so it wouldn't drift.

Wednesday–September 5, 1973

Last night Paul and Tim woke Mike to ask for a flashlight. They had seen a figure in the boat on one of their regular patrols of the property. It amazed me that they still spent almost every night up at the house. They had seen strange things almost every night. Last night, as they went toward the pond, just as they reached the runoff, their flashlight suddenly burned out. Now, it's one thing to be brave when you have a light with you and quite another in the pitch dark of a moonless night.

Mike sleepily gave them the two flashlights he had and, again, they ran for the pond. They reached the same spot in the stream and the flashlight again burned out. Luckily, Mike had given them two so, after they had crossed the stream, they turned on the other one. It didn't burn out. The boat, by this time, was drifting, empty, on the other side of the pond.

Friday–September 7, 1973

Again this morning, I found my purse moved to the same place in the bathroom and $2 missing. At least I knew where to look for it now. Moving things was not new. I remember one morning a few weeks ago we found a gallon of milk moved from the refrigerator and sitting in the kitchen sink. Then, when Mike stepped onto the back porch there was a broken rake lying with the tines pointing up. If he hadn't seen it he could have really hurt himself. These things always happened when no one was around.

Mike also found something new today. He told me to come and look in his room. He said it was foggy! When I went in, it wasn't foggy but that was as good a way as any to describe the sensation. Everything in the room was out of focus. We tried changing the lighting but it didn't help. Mike thought it was kind of funny. I didn't.

Beth's room was assailed by that awful cold again today but then a strange thing happened. Suddenly, the room filled with the smell of perfume and warmed up. It was the same scent they had smelled traces of before. It is like nothing Beth owns. I haven't smelled it as yet. Something else to look forward to! As much as I hate to experience these things, I wonder if it's the only way to be able to make sense of them.

Saturday–September 8, 1973

Last night Beth really had a strange experience. She had just turned off the light and turned over to go to sleep when she heard a drawer opening behind her. She turned to see "me" (at least a woman with reddish hair) in a long nightgown standing looking at her diary with the drawer standing open in front of her. The woman's back was towards Beth. Since she thought it was me, all she did was ask what was wrong. The woman said, "Are you sure it was June 29th?" Beth assumed she meant a fire that had taken place that day down the road and, coincidentally(?) was also the day our problems began in earnest. We had discussed the "coincidence" so Beth just said, "That's what my diary says."

At that, the woman replaced the diary, closed the drawer and walked out of the room, still with her back to Beth. Normally, I'm sure, Beth would have wondered about the long gown since I always wear pajamas. *This is just like the time I mistook the woman in a long gown for Beth though I knew Beth wore baby doll pajamas.* She should also have wondered how the woman could have read the diary since the room was dark with only the night light burning. I think it frightened her in the morning when she thought about it and realized it couldn't have been me.

Frankly, I don't even know where she keeps her diary and wouldn't presume to read it if I did. Idly, I wondered if this were the same woman I took to be Beth last month. *The long nightgown certainly fit.*

Mum and dad came today for the weekend. We sat and discussed the possible significance of "June 29th". I'm glad their visits haven't stopped because of this nonsense.

Sunday–September 9, 1973

Mum was very happy when she got up this morning. Beth's room, where mum slept, had started to get "cold" again. So cold, in fact, that it woke her up. As she lay there freezing, suddenly the room was filled with perfume and the cold receded. The only thing she could say about the scent was that it was light and floral, like a young girl's. She seemed to think it meant that one of the spirits was on our side and was trying to help us. We sure could use some "inside" help.

Thursday–September 13, 1973

Today was grocery shopping day. We have to drive twelve miles to the store so I try to shop just once a week. Beth and Mary went along to help me. All of a sudden, the car filled with the strong odor of perfume. I figured one of the girls had spilled some and paid no attention until it became unpleasant. Neither of the girls knew where the smell was coming from. They checked their purses and mine but found no perfume. Just as suddenly as it came, it disappeared.

We talked about it and suddenly it began again. The smell got so strong we had to open all the windows. If the perfume were the same as that in Beth's room, and Beth seemed to think it was, the scent was gardenia and something else. Funny, though, every time I mentioned gardenia to anyone something in my mind said "and verbena". Until I looked it up in the dictionary, I didn't know verbena was a flower used in making perfume and was especially popular long ago.

Monday—September 17, 1973

I saw a notice in the paper today that a noted psychic, Alex T, was giving a lecture on psychic phenomena on Wednesday at St. Bonaventure University. Of course, we all wanted to go and planned on it if it didn't cost too much. The last lecture we attended there only cost $.50 so I hoped this one would be the same. I made plans to contact Father Al about it.

Wednesday—September 19, 1973

Father Al called today to tell me he had good news. Not only was tonight's lecture free but Alex T had promised to come to the house afterwards. Father was very excited and explained that Alex had been called in on cases by the police in New England and that he had a tremendous psychic gift. We left for the lecture with a high degree of expectancy.

Our expectations were fulfilled. Alex took the audience, step by step through his evolution as a psychic. To demonstrate his ability, he mentally manipulated cards and dowsing rods. He also showed slides, one of which showed a ghostly hand materializing in mid-air. A series of pictures showed Alex solidifying light! It was quite incredible. They put a high powered bulb close to his eyes. He extended his hands in front of him, cupped, and soon a ball of light appeared in them. He also warned everyone that, if he shook hands with them and they were going to die soon, he would know. His accuracy at this type of prediction was 100%. Paul, who had come with us, was suddenly apprehensive about meeting him.

After the lecture, Alex was mobbed by the audience, mostly made up of students from the University. We went home and waited. It was a while before Father Al and Alex finally arrived. I was shocked when I saw how pale and tired Alex looked. He didn't waste time talking and wanted to know nothing whatsoever about the house before he checked it.

He and Father toured the house and then Alex came into the living room where we were all gathered. He sat down on a hassock and looked directly at me. Alex has the eyes of a mystic, deeply set and introspective as though they're focused on something not visible to most. In a quiet voice (I have never heard him raise his voice), he asked, "Did you know you had a mass murder here?" I guess I managed to gasp a barely audible "no".

He then explained his impressions: he saw seven spirits, some much more clearly than others—one man was stabbed (the letter opener in Mary's picture?); a woman was hanged (the bulging eyes on the woman at the pond, the figure hanging from the tree?); another woman was drowned (was the hair on the apparition at the window dirty or wet?); a man beaten to death and (here his voice broke) a young girl of eighteen with **strawberry blonde hair** was attacked, beaten and tortured to death! Like a jigsaw puzzle all the pieces seemed to fall together. It all fit so well! Too well?

He went on to explain that it had happened over a period of time about 100 years ago. The former owner of the house and, indeed, the original builder knew nothing about the murders. He thought someone from outside used the house. He felt there was a stagecoach or carriage route nearby and passengers had stopped at the house only to be robbed and killed. There were graves nearby which we may have unwittingly disturbed. Until they were buried, the bodies were kept in the crawl space. He said when Father opened the crawl space to show him the chimney he saw bodies piled like "stacks of fire wood". We had heard him gasp on his tour of the house and had wondered why, now we knew!

He also saw an elderly woman of about ninety who had died recently. He described her and said she was not involved in any way with the murders but she knew what had happened and wanted to tell someone. The description fit the former resident who had, indeed, died during the summer. Her family had brought her up shortly after the story of the house had been in the paper. At that time, she had refused to speculate on the causes of our trouble. *As a matter of fact, she refused to speak at all.*

Just then Tim, who had come in unexpectedly from his job in an Olean sub shop, said quietly, "Hey, Paul, what about the picture we took?" Alex jumped as though he had been shot. He spun on them and asked, "What picture? You mean you got a picture?" Tim, pinned by those searching eyes, was startled. He told Alex how he and Paul happened to take a very unique picture. They had concealed the story until now because they were afraid of upsetting me!

A couple of weeks before, they had been on their customary patrol of the grounds in the middle of the night when they saw a man near the pond. They had been taking pictures around the outside of the house hoping to catch an apparition off guard but not really expecting any results. Paul had a Polaroid camera and Tim a flashlight when they started chasing the man they thought to be a trespasser.

They ran across the fields and had almost caught him when they reached the tree line. Had he continued into the woods, he could have lost them easily. Instead, he turned and threw himself against a tree with his hands raised above his head. Paul, thinking of identifying a prowler, raised his camera and took a picture. Tim, who was about six feet behind the man, lunged at him just as he ducked around the tree and completely disappeared! They both realized at the same time how close they had come to the unknown and they ran all the way back to the house. Later, walking those same fields, pockmarked with woodchuck holes, I marveled that they could have run at all, especially in the dark. However, as Tim pointed out, his feet didn't have time to touch the ground!

Alex was ecstatic and wanted to see the photo right away. Unfortunately, Tim had left it at home but promised to bring it to the house the next day. Father said he'd send it to Alex and have its authenticity verified. Alex, now thoroughly drained, was visibly sagging so he and Father headed back to the University. It had been some night!

Thursday–September 20, 1973

A group of waitresses from a nearby restaurant called today and asked if they could come up to the house. Since the ridiculous traffic had died down, I said it was all right. Thus it was, that they were present when Tim and Paul brought the picture. So, at least we have some witnesses. I'm afraid it's very difficult to describe that picture. The man was middle-aged, dressed in a navy blue jacket and he seemed to be hurt. His nose was pushed to one side and his jaw was twisted. There also seemed to be either a cut or blood down the side of his face. His mouth was open in a silent scream and he was plainly terrified. Funny, though, he wasn't looking toward the boys (the camera) but behind them and to their left.

Did he see someone they couldn't? He was frightened of something but it didn't seem to be the boys. Another interesting thing: the figure had a narrow blue glow around it. It couldn't have been a reflection since the only thing behind him was a very non-reflective tree. The waitresses were as horrified as we were. There was something profoundly disturbing in that pathetic face. I called Father right away and he promised to stop by as soon as possible to pick it up.

Saturday–September 22, 1973

Mum and dad came today to spend the weekend so they, too, saw the picture. Everyone's reaction was about the same. They were shocked and almost inevitably remarked that he seemed to be hurt. Some people thought he looked like an American Indian. I didn't get that impression but, looking at the facial features, I could see why people thought so. I just wished it weren't a Polaroid so we would have had a negative. At the time, unfortunately, I wasn't aware that Bernice had a Polaroid copy machine.

Monday–September 24, 1973

Father came for the picture today. He had the same reaction we did and was very puzzled by the blue glow surrounding the figure. In psychic circles, I guess, a blue aura means a person is good. Alex told Father that after he checked the picture he would send it to the American Institute for Psychical Research in New York City for additional verification. We couldn't wait to hear their findings.

There had been a different atmosphere in the house since Alex had been here. I had often said that after a storm it felt as though the earth had been scrubbed clean. That was the feeling in the house after Alex left. I was almost afraid to hope. So far all my hopes had been dashed one by one. Could his having found out why the "spirits" were here have accomplished the miracle we had been hoping for?

Thinking back to when we had first moved in, I remembered that a barn (Alex said the bodies may have been buried near a barn) had been torn down to make room for our pond. In addition, for the first few months after our arrival, the dogs kept coming home with what I thought at the time were old deer bones. Now I wondered just what kind of bones they were and what the digging of the pond had disturbed. The pond excavation could be what had triggered the whole thing. Father kept assuring me that whatever kind of disturbance we had he could take care of it. The only thing was that he was having difficulty deciding just what our problem was. Now, with Alex's one visit, things seemed to be quieting down.

Alex had asked us to find out as much as we could about the house and to look for possible grave sites in the area. The first request was difficult to fulfill since most of the old records were unreliable to say the least and as scarce as the proverbial hens' teeth. The other was a simpler request–the teenagers from town were only too happy to help out there.

Monday–October 1, 1973

I had forgotten what peace was! It has been so quiet since Alex left I can't believe our luck. I have been checking what old records are available and found that there was, indeed, a road going quite near the house and could very well have carried coaches or wagons of some sort. The road came all the way from Cuba and wound through the mountains, passing up our road and continuing on up the route of the present camp roads. From there it must have passed the Burton Road and gone on into Olean. The boys decided that they would go and try to find out just where the old road came out.

Mike was late getting home tonight so I lay in bed listening for him. When he finally did come in I heard him slam and lock the door. Immediately after, he bounded upstairs to my room, obviously upset. Breathlessly, he told me that he and a group of his friends had gone up the Burton Road to see if the old stagecoach route came through there as the old map said. On the way up they saw a light in the trees. Stopping to investigate, they soon realized that every time they got near what they thought was the source of the strange glow, it disappeared.

As they walked, they kept encountering cold spots in otherwise balmy air and began to get very frightened by the noises coming from the woods. In their fright they decided to joke and say the sound came from "giant acorns" falling. For the rest of the time they were together "giant acorns" became their catchword. When they traced the path they were on as far as they could they saw that, strangely enough, it must be where the old road came out. Even in the overgrown sections they could see deep ruts. Mike said he had the strangest feeling someone was following him so they split up and went home.

He went on to say that he thought he had brought "someone" home with him and was afraid to go downstairs to bed. Another of our "code words". "Someone" was in the bedroom. "Someone" was in the car with me. "Someone" just rattled the cellar door. Just as he was explaining the way he felt, we heard the back door open and slam shut. He had locked it as he came in. I had heard him. Freezing in alarm, I felt my scalp crawl and Mike turned as white as a sheet. I got up and accompanied him downstairs. The door was still locked! I walked into his bedroom with him and he finally agreed he would try to get some sleep. At least they had a good idea now where the old road met the Burton. I wonder if it was worth it.

Wednesday—October 17, 1973

It has taken this long for the boys to get up their courage to go up the Burton Road again. No matter what I said, I couldn't dissuade them. This time they went up in force and figured nothing would happen. They were wrong. The trouble started with Randy, who went into a voluntary trance. Against everyone's advice, he had been experimenting with this ability and was apparently able to go in and out of trances at will. When Phil and I heard about it, we strongly discouraged him from continuing. This was a dangerous enterprise anywhere let alone in the vicinity of a "troubled" area such as we lived in.

This time, however, Mike N collapsed. He kept asking Dave to keep talking to him so he wouldn't go under. I hadn't known that Mike's grandfather had been a gifted psychic. Is it just me or is there a sudden proliferation of psychics? At that point, two more of the boys collapsed. They seemed to get worse when the moon came from behind the clouds. Those who managed to keep their awareness really had their hands full. I don't know how much of it was peer influence and how much moon influence, but the result was the same–frightening.

I told the boys later that they'd better not go up the road again if that sort of thing were going to happen. Not only did we not know what was really happening to them up there but we were in enough trouble with the townspeople already without adding to it.

Saturday–October 20, 1973

In spite of our warnings, the boys went up the Burton Road again tonight. Craig wanted to go because he didn't believe the boys when they told him what had happened. Again, they had the same problem but Craig had trouble keeping his awareness too, something he hadn't bargained for. All the boys became frightened and left except Craig and Randy. The group was supposed to meet in front of the school in town.

As Craig and Randy were driving toward town, they saw a man in the middle of the road who appeared to be headless. Craig swerved and almost ran the car off the road. Randy warned him that the next weird thing they saw should be ignored because it wasn't really there. They reached the school without further incident and began to compare notes on what had happened.

Suddenly, Clarke, Craig's younger brother, lost control of his right hand. He tried restraining it with the other hand but couldn't. Before he knew it he had drawn a figure resembling a buzz saw and a stick figure next to it of a boy–all in the steam on Mike's windshield. He was very upset about it and was afraid it would alarm Mike. They all decided at that point to call it a day. Mike was to spend the night at Craig and Clarke's house so I didn't hear of this incident until much later.

Sunday–October 21, 1973

Phil and I got up early today. Mike was supposed to come home to help Phil put insulation around the foundation of the house. We wanted to prevent our drain lines from freezing as they had a habit of doing each winter. Time moved on and still no sign of Mike. Peanuts had begun to spend the weekends with Fran and Bill, the campers directly above us, and they had difficulty getting away from him so they could go home. I took the car up the hill to pick him up hoping I'd also meet Mike. No Mike!

A few minutes after I returned home, a State Trooper came to the door and told us Mike had been in an accident and was in Olean Hospital. I don't suppose your heart can actually jump to your throat. It just feels that way. Phil and I told the girls and jumped in the car. On the way down the hill we saw Mike's old car ("Henry's Revenge" [named for Henry Ford]) leaning against a tree at the edge of a thirty foot drop off. It didn't really look too bad.

At the hospital, Mike looked pale and so young lying on the table. He was unconscious, his one eye covered by a bloody bandage. The doctor told us that they didn't have the facilities to care for him there and they wanted to transfer him to the accident unit at Meyer Memorial Hospital in Buffalo. Of course, we readily agreed. They rushed Mike to the Fire Department ambulance while I made a hurried call to the girls and another to mum. She and dad would meet us at the hospital.

I still have trouble remembering the nightmare ride to Buffalo. I usually enjoyed the sight of the rolling hills, now covered with a multicolored patchwork quilt of falling leaves. This day I saw nothing but the seemingly endless road and heard nothing but the rapidly diminishing sound of the siren. We, of course, subject to speed laws, could not keep up with the ambulance.

By the time we got to the hospital Mike was being worked on by a team of experts. Mum and dad were there, badly shaken. Mike had looked pretty bad when they brought him in. *Blood was dripping from the gurney onto the floor as they wheeled him in.* Finally, one of the doctors told us he was bleeding internally so they were going to have to operate right away. They also wanted permission to do a cranial angiogram to check for head injuries. We gave our permission for the necessary procedures and then tried to settle down to wait. It's really unbelievable how slowly time can pass–and how quickly!

After what seemed an eternity, we were told they had succeeded in stopping the bleeding by removing Mike's spleen and, so far, they could find no major head injuries. They moved him to Intensive Care. After another interminable wait, we finally got in to see him. It was quite a shock. His right eye was the size of a golf ball , swollen and black and covered with dried blood. There were bruises and lacerations all over his face. He was hooked up to a respirator, an EKG machine and an IV. Without all this help I doubt he would have lasted five minutes.

It was painful to watch him. The doctor came in and told us he was responding to commands so they were hopeful that the concussion would heal without permanent damage. Though he was in critical condition, they had high hopes for his recovery.

There was a neurosurgeon in attendance and an eye specialist was coming in to see him. We decided that I should stay in Buffalo to be near Mike. Phil and dad would stay with the girls. Phil was going to bring me some clothes from home. I was still wearing the ragged jeans I had been working in.

Monday–October 22, 1973

Phil came from home today with my clothes. He drove in early to spend some time at the hospital before he had to go to work. The girls are taking care of things at home. All Mike's friends are upset about the accident and couldn't really understand how it happened. Mike's car was old and the top speed it could manage on the hill was 20 miles an hour. Phil and dad are anxious to see the car and try to figure out what had caused the accident.

The police spent a long time searching for a passenger. Mike kept asking them if they got the other guy out. *Unfortunately, they didn't know our code words. What he was saying was that "someone" was in the car with him.* Also, there was what looked like the imprint of a head in the passenger's window. Mike had hit the rear view mirror so hard with his eye that he snapped the mirror off at the bracket so he didn't hit the passenger window. Of course, rumors are flying. Was there someone with Mike or "someone"? There was no way of knowing for sure.

The people from town sent food and offered their help. Betty stayed at the house for a while with the girls and Father was keeping close tabs on the family. Dad stayed with them the entire time Mike was in the hospital.

Mike's condition had not really changed. Sometimes I'd stand watching the dial on the heart monitor and just pray it wouldn't stop. As usual, Mike was constantly moving so they finally had to tie him down. Also, as usual, his foot was tapping out the rhythm of a song only he could hear. He still responded to orders but I didn't really think he was aware of anything.

The waiting room for Intensive Care has got to be one of the saddest places I have ever been. One woman there had a son who had been in a coma for six weeks. He had been injured in a motorcycle accident. She sat in the waiting room crocheting and waiting, prayerfully, for some sign of life. A couple from out of town was keeping vigil with their son who had been hit by a car. Most of the bones in his body were broken. He had just started a new job too.

Mum spent most of the day with me even though she was still on crutches and it was difficult for her to get around. I couldn't settle down to read and I don't know if I could have managed if mum hadn't been with me. We were only allowed in to see Mike for short periods and the waiting seemed endless. They took some more x-rays today but no one seemed to know what they were for.

Tuesday–October 23, 1973

Today passed slowly and there was still no change in Mike's condition. He was sweating quite a bit so at least I had the satisfaction of putting cold cloths on his head. He was semi-conscious at times and, if the nurse asked him if he needed anything for pain, he always shook his head. It wasn't long before he was in severe pain. I finally told them he was terrified of needles and not to ask him anymore. They then gave him the shots as ordered instead of giving him a choice. They brought a young boy in tonight. He's sixteen and had been in an auto accident too. His poor mother didn't know what to do. She had little kids at home and no one to take care of them. Her husband had to leave for work. She finally made the agonizing decision to go home when they assured her they would call her if there were any change in his condition.

It was hard to keep our spirits up with so much misery around. But at least Mike was alive.

Wednesday–October 24, 1973

Today Mike seemed no worse although he didn't seem better either. My days had settled into a routine. Mum still spent most of the time with me. She probably thought I wouldn't eat if she weren't there. She was right. I thought I noticed a slight improvement in Mike after supper and the nurses said his condition was "fair", the best report we had received so far, so I went home early. Phil came by on his way to work. He had a frightening experience in the house the night before.

He was trying to sleep on the couch because he wanted to be near the phone in case I had to call him. He was in that state bordering on sleep when he saw five men, *whom he described as being midgets,* come out of the door which now opened into a closet. Before remodeling, it was a second door to the front porch. Phil said the men were dressed in "Little Lord Fauntleroy" costumes. By the description, I would have called them Puritan outfits.

However, the men were discussing someone and saying, "Should we wait or take him now?" After apparently making a decision, they went out the same way they came in. Phil was in a cold sweat. This type of experience was new to him. By this time, he took it to mean that they were deciding whether Mike should be allowed to live or not. To satisfy himself, he called the hospital and was told Mike was in "guarded" condition. He had gotten much worse after I left.

I broke down for the first time. I knew I was much too tired to go to the hospital but I wanted to go anyway. Phil wouldn't hear of it. Instead, he didn't go to work but spent the night at the hospital. It was Mike's worst night. They worked on him almost continuously. Phil was only allowed in to see him for a few minutes every hour.

It didn't help our spirits to recall that the first thing we had heard on going to the hospital this morning was that the sixteen year old boy had died during the night.

Thursday–October 25, 1973

Mike was slightly improved this morning. Everyone in Intensive Care seemed relieved. The nurses all became very attached to their patients and took each sign of progress as a personal triumph for each of them, as, indeed, it was. Mike was still on the respirator and couldn't talk. The nurses had given Mike a "magic slate" and he was making some attempt to use it. After much trying, he let us know he wanted to see a girlfriend of his who was attending College in the area so we promised to see what we could arrange. I am still not sure he knows where he is.

Friday–October 26, 1973

They took the respirator off today and it was frightening to see how shallow Mike's normal breathing was. He has an oxygen mask on but keeps pulling it off, opening the cuts around his eye. It's proving to be very difficult for him to learn to breathe again on his own and he has such a sore, dry throat he still can't talk.

We heard that some of his friends, including Tracy, the girl he had been asking for, were coming in on Saturday with Father Al.

After looking at Mike's car. Phil and dad said that a rod had slipped loose and jammed his wheel in a left turn position. There was no way he could have avoided the accident.

Saturday—October 27, 1973

Today Mike's company came. They had to go in to see him in shifts. No more than two visitors were allowed in at a time. He was so glad to see them, although he couldn't say much. I think they were all shocked to see how bad he looked. Like us, they probably saw the car and didn't think it looked so bad. I had a terrible time persuading him to keep his nightgown down. He wanted to show everyone his scar. He didn't seem to realize that the nightgown was all he had on. Father Al brought Betty along and she, too, wanted to see Mike. She had been a good friend through all this. After seeing Mike, we all went to mum's for a short visit and then they started on the drive home.

Sunday—October 28, 1973

It was dreary all day today, although still warm for October. I wish Mike could enjoy the fading remnants of Indian Summer. At least he seemed to be making progress now. They got him out of bed for a few minutes but it was really painful for him. I wish I could see the eye doctor because I am very worried about his sight. His eyes looks so bad! They were talking about moving him to a regular room. Tom, the boy with all the broken bones, had been moved but they had to bring him back to Intensive Care when his lungs failed. I prayed that wouldn't happen to Mike. Much as I wanted him out of ICU, I didn't want him moved before he was ready.

Monday–October 29, 1973

Today they moved Mike–to an eight bed ward! The rest of the patients were elderly men, none of them brimming over with good humor. I hope he doesn't have to stay in such depressing surroundings very long. He has developed pneumonia and therapists come in five times a day to get him to cough. He is being as uncooperative as possible and even my scolding doesn't change him. *When he didn't cooperate they had to suction his lungs, a procedure he hated even more.* The oxygen mask really cut into his eyes so I finally took it off and he seems to be breathing all right. When I asked the doctor, he agreed that the mask was no longer necessary. I remember my own discomfort when I had to wear an oxygen mask so I sympathized with his plight. At this point, Mike really began fighting everyone. He didn't want to do anything he was told. At least he had some spirit left, misguided though it was.

I talked to the nurse in charge and she said they were planning on moving Mike to a semi-private room as soon as possible. That was good news!

Tuesday–October 30, 1973

They moved Mike to another room this morning! He is all alone now but they figured it wouldn't be too long until they'd have to put someone else in the room with him. Mike had a visitor today. A boy from down the hall visited in his wheelchair. He was awaiting an operation on his legs, the third in as many years. He, too, had been in an accident. It cheered Mike to have someone different to talk to. He was getting more restless every day.

More important, perhaps, the eye doctor stopped by. At first, I didn't realize she was a doctor, she looked so young. After talking to her for only a minute, I had complete confidence in her. She's that type of person. I was alarmed at first because she said that Mike had a slight leakage in his brain. She was glad it wasn't in his eye. It sounded awful but she assured me it was all right. She told me she thought Mike's eye would be okay although he would probably have to wear glasses. I would have to get a prescription for eye drops when Mike went home and be sure to use them. *Just weeks ago (2009), Mike had to have a trauma cataract removed. It had been caused by the impact when his eye hit the mirror. Miraculously, he didn't need glasses for a very long time.* I felt a lot better for having talked to her. After she left I noticed that she had really cleaned his eye up and it looked a lot better.

Mike was cranky today and wanted desperately to go home. On the rare occasions that he was allowed to get up, he was still very weak and found it difficult to move. I told him I'd call Mary S and Keith and ask if they'd visit him. I'm not sure it cheered him up but at least I tried.

Wednesday—October 31, 1973

Halloween! The girls had sent Mike some paper sculptures of goblins and witches to decorate his room to try to make him smile. Keith and Mary S came to visit him this evening. Mary was dressed as a pumpkin, which brought a laugh even from Mike. She was embarrassed at all the attention she attracted in the corridors but I told her she probably made the day for many homesick patients. Mary is so pretty anyway, she actually looked good as a pumpkin! I wonder if Keith is aware how crazy she is about him.

Thursday—November 1, 1973

It's hard to believe that November is here already. Mike is really getting cabin-fever and wants so badly to go home. It is getting harder and harder to keep him quieted down. Tonight he had other visitors–Grace, Darlene and Susan brought Annette, a friend of Mike's who had moved to Buffalo, to see him. They all had a nice time and Mike's spirits were a lot better when they left.

I saw the neurosurgeon in the hall today and told him that Mike had been playing a "maze" game and had beaten me. He seemed pleased and then suddenly grabbed my hands and said,

"But he's alive, he's alive!" Now I realize just how close he had come to dying.

Friday—November 2, 1973

Mike said the doctor thinks he can go home tomorrow if he continues the way he has been. He's so thin. I don't think he'll ever gain back what he has lost. He has never been very heavy but he's cadaverous now. His friend, Annette, came to see him again tonight. This time she brought her mother and father. We hadn't seen them since they moved out of town some months before. What a pretty girl Annette was becoming! Mike seemed to think so too. Some of his instincts were still functioning.

Saturday—November 3, 1973

Mike came home today! Phil and I took him home with many misgivings since he still had difficulty sitting up. He hadn't gotten his stitches out and wouldn't get them out for another week. This and the weakness made him lean heavily on me all the way home. We had told his friends to wait until tomorrow to come over since we knew he'd be too tired to see anyone today. Mum and dad and the girls were delighted to see him. Almost as soon as we got in the house the phone started ringing. The kids were going to visit in small groups starting Sunday.

We just heard that the town had a Mass said for Mike while he was in the hospital and almost everyone in town attended. Ordinarily, only Sunday Mass is celebrated in the small town church, but on this occasion, it was opened up in the middle of the week. This was when Mike was at his very worst and may have helped sway the balance.

Saturday—November 10, 1973

All week, Mike's friends have been coming up to visit, cheering him up quite a bit. While his company is with him, he is witty and laughing. After they leave, though, a heavy fatigue overcomes him. I'm not sure how much of it is psychological. When he saw the incision running from his clavicle all the way to down his chest, he was very upset. The condition of his eye continues to bother him. It is still very discolored and swollen. I told him the incision would look much better once the stitches were taken out and his eye would just take time to improve. Getting his eye drops in really annoys him.

Keith is staying at his camp for the weekend. I was so grateful to him and Mary for visiting Mike in the hospital and I told him so. He confided that he was thinking of moving down here. He asked if he could board with us until the weather was good enough for him to say full time at his camp. I promised to talk it over with Phil tonight.

Clarke told us he had a very harrowing experience recently on the road although he didn't elaborate. Today, he brought a group of kids up to see Mike. After visiting for a while, they left and started down the hill. On reaching the spot where Mike had his accident, the car went into a sudden, uncontrollable skid.

They wound up at the top of a hill on the left side of the road and on the other side of a six foot wide ditch, facing UPHILL! Clarke called Phil and he had to go down, put planks across the ditch and steer the car while the boys pushed it across the very shaky, makeshift bridge. The planks lasted only long enough for the car to reach solid ground again. What on earth is at that spot? *Years later, Clarke took a picture near that same area. He was aiming for the scenery which, from that vantage point is lovely. It was autumn and the colors were spectacular. However, when he got the picture developed, there was a figure on the right side that hadn't been there (at least visible to him) when he took the shot. When you study it, it resembles either a hunched man with a backpack or a Native American woman with a papoose on her back. No comment....just mentioning it.*

Since the accident, everyone has been treating the road with much more respect than usual so I have no idea how such a thing could have happened. Phil couldn't see how a car could get into a position like that even if they'd been going 100 miles an hours.

I asked for more details about the previous incident. They told me that Clarke had been visiting the girls while I was at the hospital with Mike. He and Destry, another of Mike's friends, then left and started down the hill. It didn't take Clarke very long to realize that he wasn't steering the car! He let go of the wheel and they car skillfully negotiated two miles of winding, mountainous road with no one's hands on the wheel. Clarke and Destry pronounced it "cool". I told them they were crazy.

Sunday—November 11, 1973

Beth has decided to break it off with Jeff. She had been stalling, afraid of hurting his feelings, but she finally told him of her decision. He was very upset and kind of bitter. Besides a basic difference in religion, his possessiveness was beginning to bother Beth.

Wednesday—November 14, 1973

I took Mike into Buffalo today to have his stitches removed. The doctor was pleased with his progress and set up an appointment for a checkup in about four weeks.

Tuesday—November 20, 1973

Since Mike was really getting sick of jigsaw puzzles and TV, it was a relief when some of his friends decided to spend the night. I have always bragged that the eerie phenomena always stopped when I entered the room. As usual, (especially in this crazy house), I should have known better than to speak too soon.

Mike called me downstairs after the boys had supposedly settled down on the living room floor for the night. He told me to look at Mike N. They had had nothing whatever to drink, and yet Mike N appeared to be very drunk. He changed personalities from one minute to the next. I know that when I went upstairs to bed not five minutes before, he had been fine. Now he was reeling drunkenly, pounding against the closet door and saying, "Tell them to stop talking about me." This was the same door from which the men had appeared to Phil.

Everyone thought it was funny. I didn't. I told him to settle down. He was smoking a cigarette and just flopped down on the floor. I said if he weren't more careful he'd set the house on fire. Just as I said that, the ashtray slid three feet across the floor to stop right in front of him. Without batting an eye, he put his cigarette in while the rest of us gaped in astonishment. One more thing I couldn't brag about any more.

Saturday—November 24, 1973

This evening Jeff drove up to show us his new car. It was a late model VW and was in very good shape. He was so proud of it, although he made a point of saying he bought it to take Beth out. Obviously, he doesn't want to accept their breaking up.

Sunday—November 25, 1973

This morning we had a very shattering phone call. Jeff had an accident last night on his way home from our house. It was raining and he had just crossed a one lane bridge when the car went into a skid, hit a tree and overturned. Jeff was thrown out of the car. It was quite a while before he was found on the back country road.

Beth, Phil and I went straight to the hospital. Jeff was in Intensive Care in the Olean hospital and could have no visitors. He was still undergoing tests to determine the extent of his injuries. We stayed for a short while but left when Jeff's father promised to call if there were any changes. Beth decided to stay for a while longer and Jeff's father promised to drive her home.

Monday—November 26, 1973

Jeff's condition is deteriorating. The doctors found two small skull fractures and wanted to operate. Because of his family's religious beliefs, he couldn't have a blood transfusion so an operation was out of the question. There was talk of transferring him to a hospital in Buffalo. The hospitals in this rural area are not equipped to deal with severe injuries.

Tuesday—November 27, 1973

With considerable relief, I heard that Jeff was being transferred to Buffalo today. Beth asked if she could take a week off school and stay in Buffalo. She wanted to help take care of him. Since her grades are very high, I gave her permission. She's going to stay with mum and dad, who are always glad to see her. Beth knew that Jeff would not remember their breaking up and she thought he needed the morale boosting her presence would give him. I agreed.

Wednesday—November 28, 1973

The house seems very quiet without Beth. Maybe part of the quiet was also due to everyone's awareness of the second serious accident within a short five week period. It was a very sobering thought that cast a pall over the house. *I was getting paranoid about anyone driving in the area.*

Sunday—December 2, 1973

I went into Buffalo to pick Beth up today. Jeff's parents called me during the week and told me how grateful they were to Beth. Because she was always there and willing to help, they didn't have to hire a private nurse.

Before we left, I stopped in to see Jeff and was shocked by his appearance. Beth said he looked 100% better than he had. He was virtually blind, both eyes blackened and he had many contusions and abrasions. Jeff's eyes were weak anyway but the accident made them, temporarily at least, much worse. I recommended Mike's eye doctor to Jeff's parents since Mike's eye had improved so much under her care.

Jeff really hated to see Beth go. It was going to be hard for Beth to remind him that they had broken up. *Later, we visited Jeff at home. He confided in me that just before the accident his windshield had been covered by "balloons". He panicked and swerved the car. The balloons had faces.*

Tuesday—December 4, 1973

Beth's complaints about the voices at her window had resumed and, since she returned from Buffalo, were becoming more frequent and alarming. She said she could now make out some of what they were saying. It was a man and a woman talking. Occasionally, the talks would be punctuated by "someone" hitting our oil storage tank, also outside the window–hard! This, even I heard. What really alarmed Beth the most was that they had started calling her by name.

Her stomach had really been acting up lately. *I wonder why!* So I made an appointment for her to see the doctor. No wonder she was sick!

Saturday—December 8, 1973

A group of boys stayed overnight tonight and witnessed a very frightening event. They had all crawled into their sleeping bags and cots and started to settle down for the night. Suddenly, Beth walked out of the bedroom, glassy eyed. She went into the kitchen and sat on the floor, leaning against the front door. *I am told this door is no longer there. It was a few feet from Michael's room and led to the porch.* Mike, figuring she was walking in her sleep–although she had no such history–gently led her back to bed.

A few minutes later, out she came again, this time kicking everyone in sight. She sat on the couch, extended her arms and began fondling what seemed to be a large ball, invisible to all except Beth. She kept crooning, "It's all mine. Mama gave it to me. It's all mine. So pretty!"

When the boys tried to divert her attention, she went into the bathroom and began a motion resembling kneading bread, over the bathtub! We found out much later that the bathroom had once been a pantry.

By now, the boys were following her closely, worried about disturbing her. She tried to get out the back door and, when they stopped her, she fought like a wildcat. When they finally got her calmed down, she went into her bedroom and tried to climb out

///

the window. Again, they grabbed her and made her sit on the cot in the living room.

I must explain–the cot was made of heavy aluminum, was fairly new and had heavy duty springs. It had easily held many heavy people. We always used it when we had company. Beth weighed 110 pounds and yet, when she sat down on it, it bent and both sides cracked and broke.

At this point, Mike woke Phil and me. We raced downstairs and found her in a daze. She sat, quietly sobbing, on her bed. Phil told me to take her to bed with me and he'd sleep in her room. She was trying hard to laugh at the incident but, since it was a complete blank to her, wasn't having much success. She was very embarrassed. The report that bothered me the most–during the whole episode Beth's brown eyes were a very definite blue!

Tuesday–December 11, 1973

I took Beth to the doctor today. He advised her to take it easy for a while and to take antacid for her stomach. If that didn't help, he would send her in for x-rays. I didn't mention the strange incident of the other night. I was afraid he wouldn't believe me and I think it would have further embarrassed Beth. If only she didn't hear those voices outside her room every night! She refused to leave her room. She said that they made Mary give up her room but she wouldn't allow them to force her out of hers. I thought perhaps I'd better spend the night in her bed some night and see if I could hear her "friends".

Mike had an interesting thought. He wondered if he hadn't led her back to her room when she sat quietly on the kitchen floor if it would have prevented the incident. He reasoned that whatever had led her out of her room that first time had meant to protect her. He had led her right back into the malevolent atmosphere of her room.

Wednesday–December 12, 1973

Two boys from town stopped by today. I had never met them before. They had heard that Alex had wanted us to look for grave sites in the area and they were volunteering to do just that. I think the real reason they were so willing to help was that the one boy had just gotten his car and probably wanted an excuse to drive it around. I confirmed what they had heard but told them they were strictly on their own. I'm not about to start "sponsoring" searches. *Hindsight: I probably should have forbidden them to go but I don't think it would have done any good. They were anxious for an adventure.*

I learned later this evening that the two boys had an accident on the Burton Road. The car went off the road and turned over. No more volunteers!

Sunday—December 16, 1973

Craig came to visit today. He had joined the Air Force and was home on leave for the holiday. His friends were happily chauffeuring him around to visit everyone. I asked the boys to take Pam, Laura's girlfriend, home. She was going to spend the night and needed to pick up her pajamas. Pam lived with her mother and step-father in a small trailer near where Mary, Bob, Matt and Pat had lived before moving to Buffalo. The trailer is visible from our house and sits high on the hill opposite us. Laura, Mary and Pam got in the car with Mike, Randy and Craig. On the way back from Pam's house, just as they passed the old barn near the entrance of our road, Craig suddenly cried out, "Where are the horses?"

When they pulled into our yard, Craig left the car and started toward the pond. *Remember—a barn once stood on the site of the pond.* The boys tried to stop him but he pulled away and said, "I gotta help pa with the chores." Suddenly, he stopped; looked around in confusion and asked where the barn was. Randy told him he had passed it and led him into the house.

I looked into his glazed eyes and asked what was wrong. He said, "Where's pa?" I don't think he was really conscious of me. Phil broke an ammonia capsule under his nose and the glassy look in his eyes disappeared. He was very confused and couldn't remember anything after getting in the car. I guess Beth wasn't the only one who has been affected. Strange, they both headed toward the pond. The barn?

Tuesday–December 18, 1973

Thinking about it, we were really alarmed by the new development in the house. Seeing apparitions was bad enough but when the kids start changing personalities, it was really frightening. And dangerous! What if this change were to come over them when they were alone with no one to stop them from going to the pond? Would they drown, believing it to be a barn? Did this have anything to do with the specter who appeared there?

This evening, Dave told us that Beth had tried to kill herself twice in school today. Once, by trying to jump out the window in the girls' restroom and once by trying to strangle herself in the chorus room! Most of the other students thought she was kidding but Dave had been at the house when she went "out" before. He said she had been acting strange when he saw her in the morning so he decided to watch her.

He was in most of her classes but he obviously couldn't follow her into the girls' restroom so he asked her friend, Mary K to watch her when he couldn't. Mary stopped her from jumping out the window and Dave pried her hands off her throat. Again, her eyes were glazed and "funny" although they didn't notice a change in color this time. What the hell was happening?

Saturday–December 22, 1973

Tim came home on leave from the Air Force. He, too, had joined the service so we lost our outside "patrol". It was apparent that he planned to spend a lot of time at the house. It was hard to miss the fact that he liked Beth–a lot! We thoroughly approved. Over the short time we had known him, we came to like him immensely. I felt he was a perfect match for Beth. Now, if I could only convince her.

Thursday–December 27, 1973

Tim has been coming over to the house every night to visit and every night Beth managed to be out. Tonight, at last, he caught her home. We were all sitting in the living room. Beth was on one side of Tim and I was on the other. Suddenly, I caught a glimpse of Beth's eyes–they were definitely blue and she was staring at Tim. I said, "Beth, is that you?" I had my doubts by this time. She didn't answer. Tim turned toward her and said, "She's looking at me!"

Beth had the strangest smile on her face. Her lips were in a straight line across her face and they bent up only at the corners. It was totally unlike her usual friendly smile. The hair on the back of my neck rose. Phil had fallen asleep on the floor. However, one word from Laura and Mary and he leaped up to get the last of the ammonia capsules. Luckily, one sniff of the noxious brew brought her out of it. She remembered nothing. I wonder if Tim will come back.

Sunday–December 30, 1973

The kids had asked if they could have a New Year's party tonight. We thought that if we did it might relieve some of the tension in the house so we gave our permission. The kids' friends came over to help with preparations. We had stipulated that those who could should spend the night rather than drive down the hill after dark. Since all the accidents, I have become paranoid about that hill.

Beth went to drag the sleeping bags from the closet for our anticipated guests. Somehow, she twisted the wrong way and hurt her back. When it hadn't cleared up in an hour, she took some muscle relaxant to relieve the spasms. At my suggestion, she also lay on the couch on a heating pad. Since she put my back support belt on, she couldn't have been very comfortable. Even so, she fell into a light sleep.

In the meantime, the boys came in to tell me they were going to Randy's house to pick up some pizza mix. Suddenly, Beth jumped up, flipped off the support belt, and declared she was going to ride along. She was very excited. I was more than a little surprised. The muscle relaxant should have made her drowsy, not overactive. Ordinarily, too, she would never have taken the belt off in full view of everybody. In spite of my objections, she said she felt fine and virtually bounced out to the car.

By the time the boys got back, they were alarmed. Beth told them she had taken ten muscle relaxants. I knew that if she had she would have been unconscious. Nevertheless, I checked the bottle and found it almost full. There was no way that ten could be missing. She came into the house laughing and talking much louder than I've ever heard her.

I told her she should lie down for a few minutes. She told me she only took the normal dosage of medicine...one. Though she tried, she was incapable of lying still. At that point, Tim arrived. I asked him to find out how many pills she had taken. She told him ten.

Without any warning, she slid off the bed and onto the floor. Tim carried her to the bathroom and tried to make her vomit. In the meantime, I called the hospital and they advised me to bring her in. Just then Phil drove up with supplies for the party. When I told him about Beth, he rushed to unload the car so he could take her to the hospital.

He carried her to the car. Tim got in the back seat with Beth and I climbed in the front with Phil. Half way down the hill, I had to get in the back seat to help Tim. He couldn't handle her by himself. She wasn't exactly fighting but she was moving around so much that it was difficult to keep her on the seat. She kept slipping onto the floor. The ride to the hospital, only about eight miles away, seemed to take an eternity.

Phil started to carry Beth into the Emergency Room and she went completely limp. They both almost fell to the ground. Tim grabbed her and she immediately went as stiff as a board. She continued with the same behavior once she was finally in the examining room. One minute she was lucid, the next she was almost incoherent, seemingly speaking a different language. Her stomach was pumped and they found no sign of drugs. No drugs! And yet, her brown eyes were blue!

Finally, the doctor--frankly and openly baffled--decided to keep her overnight for observation. The attendants tried putting her in a wheelchair to take her to her room. Again, she stiffened like a board. They finally had to load her on a gurney and take her upstairs lying flat.

Mike and Keith, who had been standing by, took Phil home to supervise the party while Tim decided to stay with me for a little while. He was so upset, though, that I finally insisted that he go to the party too. He took our car and went home. I was left without transportation and would have to wait until Phil came and got me to go home.

I kept an anxious vigil at Beth's bedside until about 11:30 when Phil came to pick me up. Beth was sleeping peacefully at that point and I felt it was safe to leave her. I talked to the young woman in the next bed, explaining the situation as best I could, and she promised to keep an eye on Beth for me.

When we got home, the party was in full swing. Everyone was having a good time except Tim, who sat glumly by himself. At midnight, I got a call–from Beth! Her first words were, "Ma, I just woke up in the hospital! What happened?" the last thing she could recall was falling asleep on the couch with the heating pad on.

The kids, who had to leave, started pulling out. One of the boys got his car stuck in the snow on the front lawn so Phil went outside to help push him out. He was back in a minute, blood streaming from a deep gash in his thumb. I knew by the look of it that he would need stitches. He absolutely refused to return to the Olean hospital, too embarrassed to have to seek treatment himself. Finally, Tim and I talked him into going to the hospital in Cuba and two of the boys drove him. Six stitches later, we were all in a rather subdued mood.

Tim went to Mary's room, at Phil's suggestion, and went to bed. He fell asleep right away. Poor guy–this day would have knocked anyone out. Phil realized how upset Craig was by all the crazy things that were happening. He told him to go to Mike's room and get some sleep. The rest of the kids found room to sprawl out on the floor. The girls filled the kitchen, lying side by side and the boys did the same in the living room. We had wall to wall people!

I went to bed but noticed that Laura was awfully restless. She kept getting out of bed, her room and standing at the top of the stairs like a sentinel. I thought she just wanted to be with the rest of the kids. Suddenly, she called quietly to me, "Ma, come quick! Craig's under!"

Usually, when I negotiate the steep stairs, I am extremely careful. I have taken two falls which I could never explain because I know I didn't trip. Tonight, I forgot my caution in my anxiety and hurry to get to Craig.

I could hear the most awful banging coming from downstairs. The girls' frightened voices were high and unsteady. I started to fall. Funny, I knew I was falling and, at the same time, got an impression of Laura reaching for me. She saved me from going all the way down. To do that, she had to start reaching for me before I started to fall. How she knew is beyond me.

When we got downstairs, Laura close behind me, Phil was already in Mike's room with Craig. Craig was jammed in the narrow space between Mike's bed and his chest of drawers. Every piece of furniture in the room was dancing! Did you ever have reality suspended for a moment? I did just then.

His wardrobe, chest of drawers and his heavy raccoon's cage, not to mention his bed, were bouncing around as though they weighed nothing at all. And there was Phil, right in the middle. He was trying to bring Craig out of it. He finally opened a bottle of plain household ammonia and held it under his nose. That did the trick. As soon as he woke, the furniture returned to normal. After that, Craig slept the rest of the night in Phil's recliner in the living room, surrounded by a shaken group of boys.

Monday–December 31, 1973

We decided to leave early to pick Beth up at the hospital. Tim had to go back to the base today so he went home early too. Before we left, we asked Craig about last night. He said that he was dimly aware of what was happening but could do nothing about it. He knew it was Phil trying to wake him. Two of the boys who tried before Phil had gotten hit for their trouble. But Craig remembered, even in his trance (or whatever) that Phil had just had stitches in his thumb. Thank God he fought the impulse to hit him. He's bigger and younger than Phil.

When we got to the hospital, Tim was already there waiting to be allowed in to see Beth. We could see that this friendship was getting serious, at least as far as Tim was concerned. I was less sure of Beth's feelings since, in her more lucid moments last night, she had called for Randy. When we were finally admitted to her room, Tim kidded Beth unmercifully about her actions of the day before. Beth countered with tales of having run a wheelchair race in the halls when the aides took her for x-rays. This sounded more like our Beth.

When the doctor finally arrived, he confirmed that the tests revealed no drugs of any kind in Beth's system. Not surprising since it had been quite a while after she took the muscle relaxant that she began acting strangely. He then asked if she were the same girl he had seen the night before. He explained his odd question by stating that her eyes, which today were an obvious brown, were just as obviously blue the last time he had seen her. I had wondered why he was giving her such searching looks. When I explained the situation, he asked very seriously, "Why don't you get out of the house?" Not quite as seriously, I asked, "Do you want to buy a house, Doctor?" I don't have to tell you what he answered to that.

Tuesday–January 1, 1974

Tonight a group of Beth's friends decided to have a New Year's Party for her. I know it made her feel a little better but nothing would ever make up for missing the party she had looked forward to for so long. In addition, someone had spread the rumor that she had been rushed to the hospital after having taken an overdose of "drugs". This rumor had upset her very much. Thank God, tonight's party went off without incident.

Thursday–January 3, 1974

Mike started back to school today. I had been taking him to school every so often to talk to his teachers about making up the work he had missed. The only problem was that the next day he was unable to remember the conversation. We were a little apprehensive but there was no stopping him.

Sunday–January 13, 1974

Keith moved in with us today. He wanted to stay until the better weather arrived. He plans on getting a job and settling in the area. We had to sympathize with him because we had made the same move ourselves. I don't know how he feels about living in a "haunted house" though.

Monday–January 14, 1974

Today I was changing our bed and got a jolt. I had just bought a bright yellow and orange print sheet. As I put it on the bed for the first time, a voice, whether in my mind or actual I can't say for sure, said, "Don't you see–that's the answer!" I stepped back and looked. The cheerfulness of the sheet against the somberness of the dark wood paneling created quite a contrast. The room seemed to come to life and the slanted ceiling didn't seem quite as ominous. Maybe color would help. I told Phil and he said it was worth a try. We decided that we would use our income tax refund to paper the rooms in happy colors. This seemed to be a quiet period in the house. We have had only the "normal" rappings and footsteps.

Wednesday–January 23, 1974

We finally decided that we'd have to buy Mike another car. He was hoping to go to college and would need dependable transportation. He had seen a bright red 1970 Maverick at one of the local car dealers and wanted us to look at it. It seemed to be a good buy so tomorrow Mike will become the proud owner.

Saturday-January 26, 1974

Today was a day I'd rather not recall. It cast a gloom on me I couldn't seem to shake. This morning Phil and I drove to Buffalo for a preliminary hearing about my accident. Mum and dad were at the house for the weekend. The hearing went all right but on the way home my neck began to pay the price of the long drive. I lay down in a rather cramped position on the front seat. Almost immediately I had a "dream". I shouldn't really call it a dream as I could still hear the drone of the motor and feel the motion of the car.

As clear as day, I saw the door to Mike's room draped in black and a red car, which I took to be a VW, similarly draped. I felt I had to get the draping off so I pulled at the material on the door until it fell. Then I reached for the black still covering the car and Phil's voice cut through saying, "What's wrong with your hand?" It was clutching at thin air. I explained what I had seen but was very sorry he called me before I got the final drape off.

When we reached home I told everyone about my strange "dream". They were puzzled and had the same feeling of impending doom I did. I decided to lie down for a while in the hope that the pain in my neck would ease up. While I rested the next strange event took place.

Mike had taken his Maverick to the garage in town to have the brakes checked out. In the house were Phil, mum, dad, Keith and the girls. Suddenly, mum saw Mike's car drive up to the driveway and stop. It was obviously Mike as he and his red, white and blue headband (partially covering his scars) were plainly visible. There was a woman with blonde hair sitting in the passenger seat. Mum saw the car first and, surprised that Mike didn't drive into the yard, called Phil. Phil verified that it was Mike's car by checking the license number. Just as he started to the door to check, the car backed up the narrow dirt road and disappeared. Now really puzzled, Phil asked Keith to check. He took his motorcycle and drove to town, expecting to meet Mike at any moment. He found him at the garage. The Maverick was up on the hoist where it had been for forty five minutes! Another omen! Of what? I'm still not very good at this supernatural stuff. Do I really want to improve?

Sunday—January 27, 1974

Another extraordinary event in a string of extraordinary events! In a desperate attempt to contact Alex when we failed to reach him by telephone, we had tried concentrating on him in the hopes that he'd hear us in some way. I was still very new at this kind of thing and frankly, had no faith whatever in his "hearing" us. However, our concentration bore fruit. Tonight, Alex called us!

We were sitting in the living room, trying to concentrate on getting a message to him when the phone rang. He had just landed at the Boston airport and said he had an overwhelming compulsion to call. At the very time I was talking to him, Randy was in the living room, supposedly in a deep trance, and he seemed determined to attack Paul.

Alex said he had "flown" over the house. For a moment, his words baffled me. Then I realized he meant astral projection. He said he saw influences and possessions. Even in my skepticism, I had to admit he seemed to know what he was talking about. He said he was trying to get someone to sponsor an investigative trip to the house but had been unsuccessful so far. After I confirmed his suspicions regarding the problems we have been having, he assured me he was going to intensify his efforts. In the meantime, he promised to send something of his own that we could use as a protection. He was especially worried about Beth, stating that she was the one in the greatest danger and I had to agree. I hadn't told him of Beth's changes of personality but he seemed to know anyway. Since his presence had calmed the house before, he felt that some personal possession of his would protect us.

After talking to him I had to go in and help rescue Paul who seemed in imminent danger of being strangled by Randy. I no longer take Randy's "trances" very seriously. Maybe I'm wrong but it seems to me that it's a good way to get attention and commit mayhem without worrying about the consequences. Maybe I'm just getting cynical.

Tuesday—January 29, 1974

Well my doubts about Beth's voices disappeared tonight. Earlier today I had called and made an appointment for stomach x-rays for Beth. She still wasn't feeling well. An appointment had been set up to take the tests on Thursday.

This evening I sat in the living room reading. Beth was in her room listening to records and Keith went in to talk to her. They were in full view of everyone in the living room so I caught Keith's frantic signal right away. Beth wasn't looking at him but staring into space., dreamy-eyed, lost in the music. Keith was motioning me to come in and also to keep silence. As quietly as possible, I went into her room.

My hair stood on end! I could hear two distinct voices. The one, a male voice, said, "What'll we do now? She's taking her to the doctor." The other, a woman's, replied, "I don't know. It's easier when she's sick." I couldn't tell if it came from outside the window or from the cellar stairway which would have been on the other side of Beth's wall. I motioned for Keith to stay. Quietly, I checked both the cellar (it was hard to force myself to open the door) and outside her window. I found nothing.

I returned to the house where Keith told me that the voices had continued for most of the time I had been gone! I had not heard them, either from the cellar door or from the outside tank. I clung to the thought that maybe whatever Alex sent would help. It seems superstitious to me, but anything, at this point, is worth a try. It's hard to keep your skepticism in such an atmosphere.

Thursday—January 31, 1974

Well, thank God, Beth doesn't have an ulcer. A minor miracle! Her problem was diagnosed as an extremely nervous stomach so we're really back where we started from.

Phil's car had been acting up lately so it gave him an excuse to ask to borrow Mike's car. The twin "warnings" last weekend had been preying on his mind. He thought he'd see how it handled on the long drive to Buffalo when he went to work. Mike reluctantly gave him his permission. About four o'clock in the morning, Phil called. He had an accident just outside Franklinville. While traveling south on the twisting, narrow road he had seen a tractor trailer coming straight at him in his lane. He swerved off the road but, on the steeply sloped shoulder, the little Maverick was not heavy enough to right itself. After going into a skid, it then rolled over three times across the road, landing upside down in a farmer's field.

Several trucks passed and, though he honked the horn asking for help, no one stopped. There's a truckers strike on and there had been a lot of violence so I guess that's the reason the "knights of the road" ignored him. He finally managed to squeeze his way out the passenger window and walked a mile to the nearest house. He was ignored though he could see people inside.. He walked the other way and finally came to a house whose owners were a little more humane. I promised I'd be right there to pick him up.

One of the hardest things I've ever had to do was to tell Mike his new car was wrecked. He and Keith went with me to pick Phil up. After a quick check at the hospital, we took him home with orders to rest. Now I knew what the dream meant. Somehow, I think it would have turned out differently if I hadn't gotten the drape off Mike's door. And I no longer care who called me superstitious!

Friday–February 1, 1974

Today we went out and picked up some cheery wallpaper. Dad and Gordon came down to begin the papering. Since Beth's room seemed to hold the most danger, that's where they started. How ridiculous–to fight "ghosts" with wallpaper! Next would be the kitchen, which we had been told had the most spirits and the bathroom which held the infamous root cellar door. We opted to do the rest of the house as we could afford it. Mary's room we had given up on and we seriously doubted that wallpaper would help so we put that on the bottom of the list. What a difference it made in Beth's room. No more dark corners! It was now a light and cheerful young girl's room and Beth loved it.

We received Alex's talisman today–a large lock of his hair! I guess you can't get much more personal than that. I put some in my I.D bracelet for Beth so she could always have it with her. *Recently, I found the bracelet. It had been misplaced in all our moves. The hair was gone. Either it got lost along the way or Alex took it with him when he died. Either is possible.* Alex had warned me that someone would try to make her take it off but to tell her not to listen. She promised me she'd keep it on.

Monday–February 4, 1974

Chalk up another one for Alex! Just as he had predicted, Beth's gym teacher told her to take her bracelet off. Beth knew they were allowed to keep their watches on and the bracelet had an expansion band and fit close to her wrist like a watch. She refused to remove it. Uncharacteristically, her teacher became very angry and insisted. Again, Beth refused and, instead, went to the Principal. He was surprised at all the fuss and told her that, of course, she could wear the bracelet.

Unbelievably, the bracelet had an immediate effect. The voices now sounded frustrated and said Alex was with her. Even if it was only an emotional crutch, it was working. Why is it even when I have proof I feel like I'm in the Twilight Zone and don't really believe all this stuff?

Wednesday–February 20, 1974

Strange how things work out. A distant cousin of mine whom I hadn't seen since our wedding in 1955 called mum and told her about two mediums, a husband and wife team. They live in her small town, which is about half way between Olean and Buffalo. She promised to give their phone number to mum who would then pass it on to me.

Tonight I was alone in the house and began to feel a little uncomfortable. Every so often there was a loud pounding at one of the outside doors. The dogs would rush to investigate but, after the first fruitless trip, I just ignored it. Finally, I decided to call Joan, a woman I had worked with at BOCES. We were having a pleasant talk when, suddenly, I was almost overpowered by the smell of manure.

I remember thinking, "I knew Mike's room needed cleaning but really!" The odor became worse and worse until I was forced to go onto the front porch for a breath of air. Just as suddenly as it came, it disappeared. Two or three minutes passed and the odor began again, this time even stronger. I finally made an excuse to Joan and ended the conversation.

When I investigated Mike's room, I found it completely clear of any smell and yet I would have sworn the smell was pouring like a noxious tide from that room. By the time I came back to the kitchen the odor had disappeared. I went back to reading my book, pointedly ignoring the alternate pounding at the two doors and the heavy footsteps in Mary's room. I suppose I should have turned on the radio or TV to drown out some of the racket but I felt that as long as I could hear the noise nothing serious would happen. At that point, though, in spite of my apparent unconcern, if I had seen anything strange it might have been a different story!

Friday–February 22, 1974

There was an article about Father Al in the Buffalo Evening News today entitled "The Mystery House and the Exorcist". The columnist, Bob C, intended to interview Father about an exorcism but instead wound up talking about our house. What we already knew was made more apparent–we are very much on Father's mind. In the article, he gave a brief synopsis of much of what had happened at the house. Bob C has promised to relate the tale of the exorcism in tomorrow's paper. Does he know what kind of condemnatory letters he's going to get?

Tonight Mike and Beth went to the weekly Record Hop at the school. They had been gone about an hour when Keith decided that he, too, wanted to attend. He asked for and received permission to borrow Phil's car for the four mile trip.

It wasn't too long until he was home again with bad news. He had been going over a one-lane bridge on the crest of the hill going into town when a car came up the hill with no headlights on and ran right into him. The driver lived about a mile down the road from us and was already in trouble with her insurance company for her numerous accidents. Like the Maverick, the car had no collision insurance.

Saturday—February 23, 1974

Today was incredible. Mike's friends came up to help Keith fix Phil's car. They'd worked so hard I was sure they'd have it finished by the next day. For kids they really did a great job.

As promised, the second article about Father Al appeared in today's Buffalo Evening News. This one was titled "Priest at Bona Recounts Exorcism He Conducted". In it, Father described an exorcism he had performed on a young woman at the request of famous psychic investigators, Lorraine and Ed W. The couple had recently given a lecture at St. Bonaventure and were contacted about a young girl of about 20 who seemed to be possessed. The exorcism was successful.

Wednesday—February 27, 1974

Mike asked to use Phil's car tonight. Since it had just been fixed, Phil was reluctant, but, since he had wrecked Mike's car, he couldn't very well refuse. The main reason for his reluctance was the weather. It was really cold. Ice coated everything. The hill was hazardous under the best of conditions but when it was icy it took on all the attributes of an out of control roller coaster. Nevertheless, Mike took the car but was back in about half an hour. The steering would not respond on the steep, icy slope and the car slid into a tree just off the road. Poor Phil! This time I think we'll have to get a different car.

Thursday—February 28, 1974

We were in luck. Phil managed to get a car from a man in town for only $150. Not too bad and it will do for a while.

Friday—March 1, 1974

Tonight Mike's lamp was the victim. He had a very pretty cut glass lamp on his chest of drawers. We were all watching TV in the living room and the pets were all outside. Suddenly, a horrendous sound caused us all to jump. Mike's lamp had hurtled across the room and smashed against the wall. Luckily, only a small chip came out of it and, aside from another light bulb smashing, no real harm was done. Why don't they like lamps. *Or is it the light that offends them?*

Saturday—March 2, 1974

The psychics recommended by my relative kept their promise. Paul and Peggy seemed very nice and really appreciated our problem. They promised to try to help. Some of Mike's friends were here when they came so they had an opportunity to hear about some of their experiences. Peggy affected Dave strangely, though. He was extremely uncomfortable in the room with her. Finally, she said to him, "Why don't you cry if you want to?" He had to leave the room. I guess he **had** felt like crying. This type of occurrence still makes me uneasy. Wouldn't you think I'd get used to it? Our two new friends asked if they could return some evening next week with a fellow parishioner who was an excellent psychometric. Of course we said yes. Peggy also asked for something that had been "handled" by the spirits and Beth gave her the perfume bottle that had been thrown across the room on August 10th.

Sunday—March 3, 1974

At this point I must pause for a breath. It seems, in my recollections, as though nothing good ever happened at the house. This isn't true. However, the happy times seemed unrelated to the strange events and I'm afraid, in a book, might interfere with the continuity. We had many picnics, swim parties, just-for-nothing parties and, even though our lives were rather hectic, we managed to have some very memorable times.

Our garden was a source of constant joy to me and the feeling of being watched didn't seem to matter as much when I was harvesting green beans or squash. Happily, I canned and pickled and froze the products of my tiny plot of ground. In fact, as I was in the middle of pickling some undersized watermelons, the town mayor stopped in to visit. The debris on my kitchen table didn't faze him and he settled down for a chat as I continued with my chore. If it hadn't been for these nuggets of happiness we wouldn't have made it as long as we did.

Thursday—March 14, 1974

Paul and Peggy returned this evening with the psychometric. It surprised me–the girl looked so young. When they first approached her at their church, they gave her the perfume bottle with no explanation. She asked immediately why it had been thrown. Then she went on to describe the interior of our house in great detail. She even described the paneling on the ceiling, a rather unusual feature.

We told her about the lamp being thrown and were told to bring it in. After touching it the young woman said someone was very sorry such a pretty thing had to be thrown but it was to convey a message. If so, the message didn't get through. Peggy then proceeded to describe two spirits she could sense in the living room–one a woman with long skirts who was very angry looking and the other, a man, who either had his eyes blindfolded or darkened in some way. She took it to mean the man was blind. Paul took a walk outside and when he came in asked who "Anna" was. He said "someone" was standing under the pine tree calling

"Anna". He wasn't sure if she was calling someone or telling him her name. I had dismissed it before but several visitors claimed to have heard someone saying "Anna" or "Mama".

We learned much later that the daughter of one of the original owners of the house was, indeed, named Anna.

All in all, it was an interesting evening. I hope I managed to hide my doubts. All through this I saw proof, time and time again, that something extraordinary was at work and yet some perverse part of my mind refused to accept it. Part of me sat back and said, "I'll play along but I don't believe it." Maybe it was my way of staying sane.

Saturday—March 23, 1974

Bob C's column proved what I had expected. This article was titled "A Mailbag Potpourri: Barnum, Nixon, Sinatra". The only part that interested me was the criticism of Father Al. The writer of the letter quoted Barnum's famous adage about a sucker being born every minute and stated boldly that Father Al was a sucker for believing in our story. Bob C answered by defending psychics in general; Father Al in particular and us by association. He explained that men and women in the field of psychic phenomena are dealing with the mind, a relatively unknown area and stated that they received little reward or credit for their achievements. He went on to state how happy he was to have had the chance to meet men like Father Alphonsus, who contributes more to mankind in a day than Barnum did in a lifetime. Bravo!

Friday—March 29, 1974

The Buffalo Evening News carried another article about psychic phenomena today. This one was titled "Probing the Psychic, Unknown Can Pit Spook Against Spoof". As usual, the columnist was Bob C As we expected, he is receiving all kinds of letters, many of them derisive and derogatory. One, however, had been sent by one of our camping neighbors. Ann and Lee T and their twins were good friends of ours. In the letter he stated: "I was once an unbeliever but now I am convinced. When you sit out in the field at night and your hair stands up and you feel you are being watched and can't see anybody or anything, no matter how powerful a flashlight you have, you know something strange is present.

"I hung a cross in my garage and it was thrown to the floor a few times. I have no explanation for that. I am not one to be afraid of anything, but I know something is there. I have no intention of leaving the place and will fight back with any weapon I can get."

Another letter was one from me thanking him for defending Father Al against the scoffers, who are legion. A third was interesting to me because it was a quote from a fellow friar from St. Bonaventure's. he had apparently been present when Alex T returned from his visit to our house the night of his lecture at the college. In it, he stated that Alex was "so badly shaken, I thought he might have to be hospitalized. This is not my field but after seeing (Alex) T I believe the stories I have heard about the house."

Well, at least everyone isn't skeptical.

Monday—April 1, 1974

April Fool's Day! I got a long distance call from New York City today. A girl named Jan, who is a student at New York University said she would like to come down with Alex and film the story of the house. They would bring a film crew with them. The project was supposed to be sponsored by New York University, Educational TV and the Institute for Psychical Research. I agreed and a tentative date was set–April 12. Maybe things would soon be better. Alex was coming.

Saturday—April 6, 1974

Beth left for Chicago today. Tim wanted her to spend Easter with him. He had only a little time off but he wanted her there. She was to stay with friends of his. Beth and Tim's friendship had come a long way and everyone knew they'd want to get married soon.

Sunday—April 7, 1974

Mary and I decided to walk up the camp roads today. On the way up, Keith's trailer was clearly visible. Some of the boys had stayed overnight with him so we half expected to see them. Since the weather had begun to warm, Keith had been staying in the trailer instead of at our house. The rear door of the trailer was standing wide open. We could see Randy sitting on a kitchen chair, his elbows on his knees, staring at us. He was right in the doorway. It would be hard to mistake him for anyone else since he has silver-blond hair which, on this day, almost glowed in the brilliant spring sunshine. We shouted to him but, instead of acknowledging, he got up, picked up the chair and walked away.

I was puzzled and could think of no reason for his actions so we decided to investigate. After knocking a few times on the door (which was now pushed to) and waiting perhaps five minutes, a very sleepy looking Dave came to the door. I asked where Randy was. He said that they had to take him home last night because he was sick. I asked who else was in the trailer. He replied that only he and Mike N were left since Keith had taken the other boys home and hadn't returned as yet. I told him what we had seen. He turned white and went to wake Mike N. He was equally sleepy and equally puzzled. The only exits had been plainly visible to us all the way up the hill. We checked the trailer and found no one else there. What's the point?

Thursday—April 11, 1974

Tim called today to ask if Beth could extend her stay until Monday. He didn't want her at the house when Alex came for the filming. He was afraid of the emotional upset it might cause her. I could understand his concern although I felt Beth was made of sterner stuff than he realized. We finally decided to let her stay.

Friday—April 12, 1974

All day today we stayed close to the phone not knowing what time Alex and his party would be arriving. It was late, about 10 p.m., when we finally heard from them. They were at a truck stop about eight miles from the house so I drove out and led them in. It would have been impossible for them to find their way up the unlighted, twisting back roads. There were three cars of them and with the exception of Alex and a representative of the Institute, they were all about college age. Jan was the only girl. They had coffee and homemade doughnuts, unloaded their equipment and, after a cursory look at the house, left for the motel in town. The motel was owned by Eddie G's father so they would get a discount. Eddie is one of Mike's classmates *and the star of the Hinsdale basketball team*. The brave little group would be back in the morning. As I got ready for bed, I wondered if they knew what they were getting into. *On the other hand, I wondered what would happen if whatever haunted this house would refuse to cooperate. I'd hate to have wasted their time. It would be just like our resident spooks to go on strike at this point and refuse to respond.*

Saturday—April 13, 1974

Well, our guests were here bright and early. I was afraid Alex would wind up bald as they taped a lock of his hair on every piece of equipment they had. That is, they thought they protected every piece but inadvertently forgot one of the camera lights in Beth's room. Father arrived to assist in the proceedings. We were told to take the kids and disappear for a few hours as they thought things might get dangerous. We obliged.

We came back about supper time and everyone was very excited. In Alex's attempts to clear Mary's room he wound up with a small burn on his back. Father had to hold him up as his strength was seriously depleted in the encounter. He said a young woman had died in that room and didn't want to leave. He felt she had been locked in the room for a long time before she died. However, he was sure he had been able to convince her otherwise. We were to be a part of the filming tomorrow. I learned from Jan later that some of the men in the crew were so emotionally keyed up by the events of the day that they actually burst into tears when they returned to the motel.

In the meantime, the inner man had to be fortified, ghosts or not, so I made a huge pot of spaghetti. We all sat down to eat when Jan asked what the delicious drink was. It was water from our well! She never knew water tasted like that. So much for New York City water!

Sunday—April 14, 1974

Today we filmed interviews with our family and friends, including a description of Beth's breaking the cot, a walk up the road to the "hanging tree" and Alex's explanation of that particular phenomenon and, finally, the ceremony to rid the house of our unwanted guests. During one interview, filmed in the living room, the one camera light suddenly fell and smashed, narrowly missing Paul. It was the lamp they forgot to "protect" with Alex's hair.

The interview about the cot was filmed on the front lawn and the soundman had a bit of trouble because of the wind. We then walked down the road to the old shed. The scene at the "hanging tree" there surprised even me. As Alex and I approached the tree I told him that the branch I had seen the "body" hanging from had long since fallen and was piled with the multitude of other limbs, victims of wind and ice. I knew which branch it was, yet without my guidance, Alex walked directly to it and said, "This is the one, isn't it?"

He then said the woman, about 21 years old, was hanged by the inhabitants of a house only a short distance away (not our house). He then pointed directly at a thicket which I knew contained the foundation of an old house. There was no possible way he could have known it was there. He said the woman was traveling by coach to meet her husband in Pennsylvania and that she was expecting a child. The residents in the house, which was used as a kind of way-station, branded her a "scarlet woman" and executed her. He thought they were members of a fanatic religious cult.

Later, when her husband came looking for her, they refused to tell him where she was buried so he planted two sections of daffodils in her memory. In the wooded area just near the old barn were, in fact, two circular patches of daffodils which I had never noticed before. He also said there was a stream nearby with strange blue feathery flowers above it. The water fell into a pool and, if you listened, it sounded like the water was whispering the name "Clarice". There is such a stream in the gully near the road. The feathery flowers were not yet blooming but would appear among the elderberry bushes in June. I don't know how he knew about them. I never did listen to the stream.

While Alex was still at the tree talking to the crew, I walked across the road and climbed a small rise overlooking the whole scene. I guess I was trying to picture what the movie would be like. I was only half listening and could hear wind gently rustling through the leaves of the apple tree behind me.

Gradually, without my being aware of it, something changed. I felt as though I were in a different world. I looked down and saw, not my jeans but a long, blue patterned dress and brown, old-fashioned shoes. I was no longer in the field but stood on rough boards and I was terrified. I could hear someone yelling at me. I don't know what, I only knew the words were hitting me like fists. It only lasted a moment and then I was back on the hill watching Alex. Just then Pam's mother, Charlotte, came down the road and called to me. She asked if I were sick as I was very pale. I didn't tell her what had just happened.

Later, Alex gently asked me if I had undergone some type of experience out on the road. When I told him he said that often happened when he was around and not to worry about it. Not worry about it?

In the evening, the family knelt in the center of the living room floor with Father Al and Alex and we all held hands. First, Alex drew all negative powers present into himself and dispelled them and then Father Al read the Church's simple exorcism rite. When they were finished we expected to be able to rise. My knees were beginning to give out (I never was a very good kneeler) and I began to have visions of fainting dead away (nothing ghostly about these visions).

Glancing surreptitiously around, I could see no one else in the circle was in much better shape. We were all wobbling and still the cameraman did not tell us to break. Finally, when we had all about given up, they told us to relax. It seems that during Alex's ceremony and the whole time Father was performing the age-old exorcism rite there were horrible screams and groans outside which seemed to be coming from the house itself. They continued to roll the cameras (and the sound equipment) for as long as the incredible sounds lasted. Well, it certainly was an interesting ending to a very interesting weekend. But who screamed?

Monday—April 15, 1974

I drove into Buffalo today to pick Beth up at the airport. It was good to see her and from her radiant face it was easy to see she had a good time.

There was a sense of complete peace in the house and for the first time in years the place seemed normal. It was a good homecoming for Beth. Perhaps the best proof of the change in atmosphere–Mary moved back into her room.

Tonight for the first time since Alex left, I had time to think. It rather upset me that he had changed his first diagnosis. The first time he came, he picked up so many spirits we had seen and the deaths seemed to fit so well with the signs we had been getting. Was he wrong the first time? Remembering the look of shock on his face then and comparing it to his almost jovial attitude during the filming, it was hard to believe. What was really frightening was the nagging thought that perhaps he had been wrong the second time. What if whatever was here was manipulating him? Was that possible? Were they able to fool him? In that case, was the welcome respite only temporary *or worse, an illusion?* I felt like Damocles! I wish there were some foolproof way of knowing. *Over time I have come to believe that different entities enter the area at different times. I think the person experiencing the phenomenon affects what they see and how they see it. Guest ghosts?*

Friday—April 23, 1974

Once again, we were written up in the Buffalo paper. This time Bob C's column was titled "That Old Haunt In Hinsdale Got a Large Share of Exorcize". He has a flair for titles. This commentary synopsized Father Al's audio tape about the exorcism that took place over the weekend. The details were pretty accurate since most of it was quoted verbatim. If this experience has taught me anything, it's that reporters don't always hear what you're trying to tell them. Maybe they feel obliged to put their own spin on things. Hopefully, this will be the last article we'll have to deal with.

Wednesday—April 24, 1974

Today Tim called long distance and asked if he could marry Beth. She had been supposed to ask us herself but had been afraid we'd be angry. I promised to talk to Phil but I was sure he'd approve. We only worried because they were both so young. The reason they were in such a hurry was that the Air Force was transferring Tim to California in August and they didn't want to be separated. Instead of a May wedding, which she had initially requested, I talked Beth into setting the date in August. We decided on August 3, the day before Tim's nineteenth birthday. Beth would be only seventeen.

I didn't say anything but the thought of how we would pay for the wedding was already worrying me. Phil had finally taken the big step and changed to a job in Olean. It paid much less than Ford so he was also tending bar part time in town. Even with the two jobs our income had dropped drastically.

Saturday—April 27, 1974

Beth has already asked the girls who were to be her bridesmaids. Pat P was to be Maid of Honor, Mary K and Tim's sister, Diane, her bridesmaids, Gary her ring-bearer and Michele her flower girl. The attendants were going to make their own gowns and I would make Beth's. The girls were already planning a shower for Beth in July.

Friday—May 3, 1974

Mike has decided to join the Navy. He has been mulling it over for some time. Tomorrow will be his eighteenth birthday and he will leave for the Navy right after graduation. He has settled on a career in Nuclear Energy so he had to sign up for six years. Phil and I felt he was making a mistake. For one thing, it was too soon after his accident and he was still having trouble with his memory. For another, he hadn't allowed himself sufficient time to think it over. However, we couldn't really afford to send him to college so we resigned ourselves to his leaving. *In the back of my mind was the nagging fear that he had committed himself to escape from the house and its malevolency.*

Sunday—June 2, 1974

The days have been passing in a welter of activity. We have met Tim's family and discovered kindred souls. We have shopped for patterns, material, flowers and accessories. Today was Beth's first shower. Cathie and Mikki gave it for her in Buffalo and most of our relatives attended. She got beautiful gifts.

Saturday—June 15, 1974

I have decided we just can't afford a big wedding. Again, our long suffering friends and relatives are coming to the rescue. They offered to bring food to the reception so we won't have to hire a caterer; one friend got a discount at a hall in Olean; two of the boys offered to act as photographers; and the kids' friends are providing the music. Father Bob is coming in from Buffalo to perform the ceremony.

Monday—June 24, 1974

Mike is gone! It seems unbelievable. Yesterday he graduated as salutatorian of his class and today he's gone. He wanted to sneak away so he went to the bus stop alone. However, one by one his friends spotted him so that by the time the bus left the driver must have thought he was a celebrity he got such a send-off. He felt bad, though, about missing Beth's wedding.

Tuesday—June 25, 1974

Laura didn't waste any time. She moved into Mike's room before it was cold! Her old room was so small I didn't really blame her for feeling anxious. Mary is planning on moving into Beth's room as soon as she's married so this summer will bring a lot of changes.

Sunday—July 7, 1974

Today was Beth's shower. Her bridesmaids held the party at Mary K's home. The weather was so beautiful we were quite comfortable in the copse of trees all decorated with crepe paper. We really had a wonderful time and, again, she received beautiful gifts. I say this in spite of the fact that Mary K's dog mistook my purse for a fire hydrant.

While we were having a good time, Phil ran out of gas going up the hill on his way home. He walked to the house and arrived out of breath and annoyed with himself. He had to get ready for his second job. He ran upstairs and stopped, dumbfounded, at the door of our room. A book was floating in mid-air, about three feet above the dresser. For a moment he didn't move. As he watched, the book dropped slowly to the bookcase next to the dresser. It was the Rubáiyát of Omar Khayyám.

Later, when he told me about it, I could think of no message that particular book might have. The marker was at the passage, "The moving finger writes...etc., right where I had left it. This verse could be applied to any situation and didn't seem to be a message. With a weary sigh, I wondered if it were starting all over again.

Tuesday–July 10, 1974

The trouble **had** started again. Laura had a terrible experience last night. Julie was sleeping with her in her new bedroom when the dog suddenly began to growl. She was looking under the bed, her hair standing on end. Laura, figuring it was one of the cats, leaned over and looked. There was a black, furry ball under the bed and the only feature visible was its mouth full of pointed teeth. The night light in the kitchen sent sufficient light into her room to make it easy to see.

Laura drew back, startled, whereupon Julie pounced on her bed, pranced around in an obvious attempt to get Laura to follow her. She then jumped off the bed and waited at the door. Laura took the hint and jumped too. As her foot touched the floor, she swore something grabbed at her ankle. She could hear snarls coming from under the bed. She sobbed herself to sleep on the couch and I knew nothing about it until morning. A very depressed young lady moved back into her old room today.

Friday–July 12, 1974

Today they're papering Mike's old room in the hopes that it will make it possible for Laura to move back in. We chose a cheerful white paper with yellow daisies and sunflowers marching in rows. It made a world of difference and seemed to bring the sun into the room. Laura has agreed to try again.

Saturday–July 19, 1974

Tonight I went to bed while Phil stayed in the kitchen talking with some of Mike's friends. There was a strange feeling in our room but I attributed it to my nerves *or imagination*. After I got into bed, I turned part way over onto my stomach. In an instant I was paralyzed! I almost panicked when I realized I couldn't move. No pain–just unable to move. I prayed, inwardly, and after a few minutes I was released.

Suddenly, Mary called to me from her room in a rather shaky voice. I asked what she wanted but all she said was "Goodnight" in a very strange voice. Just then, whatever it was hit me again. I lay there sweating and praying and wondering what, in the name of God, was happening to me. Again, I was released. I started to change positions so I could get up when, for the third time, I found myself unable to move. Now I was really frightened. I tried desperately to move and could not bring my mind to accept my inability to do so. Once again, I was freed.

Although each session could only have lasted a couple of minutes, it seemed like an eternity. I finally managed to call Phil. When I told him what had happened he came right to bed so I wouldn't be alone again. Our talking had alerted Mary. She told us why she had called to me. She had seen a young boy in jeans standing beside the TV *at the foot of the bed*, watching me. At first she thought it was one of the boys but then she realized they were all downstairs. Whoever it was watched me until I called Phil.

Saturday–August 3, 1974

A miracle–everything was done in time for the wedding. The whole day was beautiful and went off as planned. Our friends and relatives provided most of the food. We really had a full house.

When Beth and Tim went back to the house to get changed I forgot to give them the door key. I would have liked to have a picture of the groom removing the screen window so his bride could climb in!

When we returned to the house it was full of people who were unwilling for the party to end. We were up very late. The last sight I saw as I went to bed was the stream of punch flowing across the kitchen floor. I ignored it.

Tuesday—August 6, 1974

Beth and Tim came back from their honeymoon early so they could see all their friends before leaving. Tim and I were talking about their going to California and I said I'd always wanted to live there. Tim said, "Why don't you? and I couldn't think of an answer.

Saturday—August 10, 1974

The happy couple has left already and the house seems somehow emptier than it ever has. After all the activities in connection with the wedding, we felt a real letdown. This was a different quiet than before because this time I knew Beth wouldn't be back. Beth and I were not just mother and daughter but friends as well. I hope even though we're separated by space, we can retain our present closeness. *Beth's departure after Mike had also left, made the house echo with emptiness. They had been such a large part of our household.*

Saturday—August 24, 1974

Phil and I were getting worried about our financial difficulties. We had made attempts to sell the house but all to no avail. At one point a family drove from Buffalo to see the place. It just happened that a local psychic had said that something would happen that night so Paul and Father Al were present in case they were needed. Suddenly, one of our kids came running in and said, "The woman's at the birdbath!" Father and Paul ran outside. The prospective buyer said, "Oh, I saw that lady out there—she's dressed kind of funny." I must have given her an odd look because her voice trailed off and they left almost immediately. How **not** to sell a house! *It didn't help that the ad I had taken out in the Buffalo paper listed the price of the house as $20 not the $20,000 we had stipulated!*

In trying to sell the house, we made no secret of the troubles we were having. We felt we couldn't foist our problems off on someone else unless they knew what they were getting into. We were kind of hoping that a research facility would buy it and try to find out what was going on here.

We had received publicity in the Buffalo paper, as well, and, from what I heard, some out of state papers had also picked up the story. We had a call from an out of state "expose" newspaper and from a radio station requesting an interview. All this had not changed the fact that we were headed for bankruptcy.

Sunday—August 25, 1974

Mum and dad have come for the weekend. There's a heavy feeling in the house, probably caused by our sense of defeat at having to sell the house. Today I feel wiped out. My head has begun to throb. Mum told me to lie down so I wasn't present for the following event although I did hear the voices and thought it was mum talking to Phil and dad. I hesitated putting this in the original manuscript because it sounds so incredible I was afraid no one would believe it. Now, I find myself feeling the need to tell you what happened to mum. Dad and Phil were walking the grounds outside and discussing a way to make the property more attractive to prospective buyers without deceiving them about the problems they might face. They were within earshot of the house. Mum was straightening up the kitchen, more to keep herself busy than anything else. Suddenly a woman walked in the door. She wore a navy blue suit, slightly out of date and, even more anachronistic, a cloche hat. She greeted mum and said she and her husband were interested in buying the property. They sat at the table and mum answered the woman's questions about the rooms of the house. Finally, the woman rose and said she had to join her husband who was outside talking to dad and Phil. She left but mum was uneasy about the whole incident so she went outside to ask dad what the pair had said to them. Neither dad nor Phil had seen anyone—woman or man. There had been no prospective buyer, no visitor, no one. This is incredible to me and it upset mum when we showed any doubt. So, I must chalk up another first for the house. Interactive spirits?

Wednesday–September 11, 1974

Monday we picked Mike up at the Naval Base near Chicago. His boot camp training was over and he would have some time at home before his first assignment. On the way home, the water pump in our car broke and dad had to come and pick us up and drive us the rest of the way home. Luckily, it was only about twenty miles but it wasn't a very good beginning for Mike's leave.

Thursday–September 26, 1974

The car really went this time! The man who had changed the water pump had not done a good job and the engine was ruined. When we turned the key in the ignition, one of the pistons dropped right out. Just one more blow!

Saturday–September 29, 1974

We have decided to declare bankruptcy. After putting the house in the hands of real estate agents and trying to sell it ourselves, we have given up. *The house was notorious at this point and who wants to buy a haunted house?* Our many accidents and the loss of my income had also contributed to our present state and we could see no other way out. With my heart in my shoes, I promised to call the lawyer.

Friday–October 11, 1974

It's amazing how easy it is to lose everything you own. Well, it's done. The girls are set to leave with mum and dad this weekend. Phil and I are going to stay and finish up the odds and ends. The cats are going to Buffalo with mum and dad too and we are going to bring the three dogs. Paul took Pixie. Mum took Barney and Jingles. I had to give my beloved Dolly to some friends. Gypsy got the jump on all of us by leaving a couple of months ago with Jasper. Maybe she knew something we didn't. It was sad watching out little family break up.

Phil has decided to go to Ohio to stay with his family for a while and I am going to stay with mum and dad. I think Phil is an emotional wreck. All we have worked so hard for during the past twenty years is gone. His nerves have been shattered by the events in the house so I hope his staying in Ohio will help.

Sunday—October 13, 1974

The house is really quiet now. Only Phil and I remain with the three dogs–Lassie, Julie and Peanuts. Today we went to bed early. We had just settled down when a car drove into the yard. Phil jumped up and ran to the back door. There was no car–yet we had seen the lights and heard the motor. There had even been the sound of a car door slamming. He no sooner got back into bed when it happened again. This happened six more times before I could get Phil to ignore the lights and sounds. Complete silence descended.

Then, just as we started to relax, a gong started in the cellar! A real Chinese gong! And it was loud! Again, Phil raced downstairs *despite my protests*. Again–nothing. In rapid succession we were subjected to sounds of a baby crying, a whistle, a siren, bells and a repeat of the gong (I guess they ran out of sounds!). Each time Phil insisted on investigating. "They've got a baby down there–they'll hurt it! Finally, whether because of my persuasive powers or, more likely out of sheer exhaustion, he ignored the noises. Thereafter all we heard were the familiar footsteps.

Monday—October 14, 1974

We are both tired and ill at ease. Phil went to the store this morning, leaving me alone. Suddenly, someone pounded hard on the living room window, starting the dogs barking furiously. I ran outside–nothing! Feeling a little better in the open, I walked around the pond for one last time–the dogs at my side. I had just reached the other side when I heard someone call what sounded like "Mama". I looked up the hill to see a figure near a pine tree. Then it was gone. I went back to the house.

When Phil came home I said, "Don't we have somewhere we have to go?" He knew just what I meant. We went to visit Hugh and Lois, Tim's parents, in Olean. We were so glad to be away from the house. On the way home we stopped and had a sandwich at Bernice's restaurant and she insisted we stay overnight the rest of the week with her. Gratefully, we accepted. We only went back to the house to feed the dogs.

Still, I fought the feeling, as we had all fought it for so long. The house had been called so many things: evil, haunted, troubled, diseased, leprous, insane. If so, then why did I love it? Why did we all love it? Why was it so hard to leave? And so necessary?

Thursday—October 17, 1974

It was time to go. The tension grew, almost palpable in the air, making our movements hurried and uncoordinated. Slowly, the house grew colder, the cold reaching within and clutching at our midsections with a death grip. How can cold come from inside? Was it trying to hold us here or finish driving us out? We felt like mice, scurrying through a maze, never quite sure what we'd see at the end. The house was silent, waiting, making our silence even more pronounced. The boxes accumulated in the kitchen and were loaded one by one in the car. To add to the general confusion, the three dogs wove in and out, tripping us, knocking over boxes and generally slowing us down. And yet, with all this canine activity, there was not a sound—no barking, whining, howling—only silence. *I guess this kind of proves what they say about animal sensitivity. Also, I'm sure, they didn't want to be left behind.*

Finally, the last box loaded, the last dog settled, we got in the car and, with a sigh of relief, drove away. And yet, my feelings weren't all of relief but of a gnawing sense of failure and sadness. A deep, heavy feeling I have never experienced before and, with the help of God, never will again. *Strangely enough, I also felt a sense of betrayal, a sense of abandoning something—house? Spirits? Who knows?* I asked Phil to stop the car just past the driveway and looked back. The scene appeared so normal, so bucolic! I looked at the house, sparkling white, with the beautiful New York hills as a backdrop; the pond, twinkling in the autumn sun, reflecting the tapestry of the leaves, my beloved garden, now stripped and forlorn and the stately pine tree guarding the entrance to the drive. The ache in my heart started a pressure behind my eyes and I knew I would soon give way to tears. How could I leave this place? My mind screamed, "It doesn't even look haunted!" then, as I watched, the face of the house became malevolent. Was this shifting, pulsating metamorphosis in my mind or was I seeing the place as it really was? I turned to face the windshield and didn't look back again.

Thursday-October 31, 1974

Phil has gone to live with his parents in Ohio for a while. The girls are staying in one of the upstairs bedrooms. The dogs and I make our home in the attic. *The four of us sleep in a twin bed. At least I don' get cold.* The cats go wherever they want, as cats are wont to do. On an impulse, I called Bob C to let him know that we had left the house. Last Saturday afternoon, dad, Mary and I went to see him in his office for one last interview. In as concise a manner as possible, I recounted my version of what went on in the house–not an analysis, just a statement of events. Today, the interview was printed under the title: "'Spirits' Drive Buffalo Family Out of Their Home in Hinsdale". With only a few exceptions, he got the facts straight. At the end of the article, Bob C says "I know this story will bring another rash of cynical letters and I can understand the criticism. But I won't go along with it because of the people involved. Nor will I stop trying to find out more about the matter from my friend, Father Alphonsus."

Saturday-November 23, 1974

Apparently, the interest in our house hasn't died. Bob C's column today was titled "Readers Drop a Line to Get a Few Loose Ends Tied Up". In it was a letter from a reader in Silver Springs requesting an update. Bob informed the man that he was still gathering information on the house. From where?

June, 1975

Unfortunately, the date has been cut off the article in the Buffalo newspaper. As usual, it was Bob C's column and it was titled "For Rent: Nice Home in Hinsdale Suitable for Psychics, Skeptics". Another letter from a reader, this time from Cheektowaga, prompted this column. Bob relates that on June 7 he and his son had journeyed to the house. Father Al accompanied them as he knew they'd never find the place by themselves. He reports nothing new but only goes over old material. One thing I found interesting, though, he had the same idea I did. He suggested that psychic groups rent the place and do a thorough investigation. This had been my hope for a long time. A hope that was apparently never to come to pass.

Friday-October 31, 1975

Halloween seems to bring out the worst in some people. Father Al sent me a copy of an article carried in The Bona Venture, the student newspaper at St. Bonaventure University. In it, they thoroughly ridicule our family. Supposedly, "fictionalizing" the account gave them this right. Most of the details were wrong. Apparently, the reporter visited the house and talked to the current owners who also made fun of our ordeal. The new owners stated that I had said there was "blood running from a faucet". That was a blatant lie and I have no idea where they got such a preposterous notion. The owner then claimed to have cleaned the pipes of rust whereupon the "blood" disappeared. I wonder how he found the rust in plastic piping?

They also claimed I had been fired from my job at BOCES. Never in my life have I been fired from any job. If I weren't in San Jose at this point, I'd sue for libel. However, on the 15th of this month, I started a job for the City of Santa Clara in California so I'll try to put this calumny behind me. Anyway, since it's written under the guise of "fiction", I suppose I wouldn't get anywhere.

The ultimate insult, though, really made me angry. Clearly, they had found an old diary of Beth's. At the time of the trouble, if you remember, she was a teenager. Affectedly, she had signed her name "Dorcus" for no real reason except she liked the sound of the name. Dorcus has a ring to it that "Beth Ann" doesn't. The writer of the article made a big deal about it saying that "Dorcas" was a character in the bible under Acts 9:36-43. I very much doubt Beth has ever read Acts. Someday, I'll make a point of reading it myself since, according to them, it involves a woman who died in an upstairs bedroom and was raised up again. The musings in the diary were intensely personal and I resent their using the inner turmoil of a young girl for their own purposes. If they had been any kind of decent people, they'd have given the diary to Father Al who would have returned it to Beth. I'm sure she never intended to leave it for anyone else to find. Will they never let it rest? *At first, I felt guilty since I was responsible for packing things up. Beth and Tim were in California. However, I have since learned the diary was in the crawl space....a place I have never gone nor intend to go!*

Thursday—May 27, 1976

Still, the interest in the house continues. Bob C's column was entitled "Last Rites Given the Spirits That Haunted Hinsdale House". Once again, a letter from Batavia which referred to Alex T's book, *Beyond Coincidence*, prompted the article. Apparently, Bob had contacted Father Al to ask questions posed by readers. Alex's book mentioned our house and aroused a renewal of the curiosity we had become accustomed to. The questions and answers were a re-hash of everything that had already been said. One exception this time was a comment from Bob himself. When asked whether we could have moved the bricks in the crawlspace, Father had said that it was virtually inaccessible. Bob said, "I had a chance to see the small 'attic'–really a crawl space as Father T calls it and will say that only a small acrobat could get to its entrance and through the opening without a 6-foot plank." Will this article mark the end? One can only hope.

Clara M. Miller

Sunday—October 27, 1985

I have in front of me an article from a magazine which I cannot identify. It is titled "Encounters with the Supernatural" from a column by Jane K called *People Talk*. The piece is about Father Al and features a very fetching photo of him holding a skull. The photographer must have been very talented to make a mild, gentle looking man like Father Al appear even remotely menacing.

Once more, our house is mentioned. The article is tongue-in-cheek and, at last, gives readers a hint of the humor that characterizes our friend, Father Alphonsus. When asked if he has any plans for Halloween, he answers, "I invite over a lot of very, very friendly spirits. Those that come into my classroom every day, and some poltergeist spirits, some deceased friends that I know very well. We have a good time–talk over old hauntings together and see what's new in the spirit world. Only kidding."

I have a copy of another article, apparently from a rotogravure section of the Buffalo Courier-Express. I'll let the last few lines say it all. "The house had won. Father T said he could not find any simple normal explanation for what took place. 'It was really a haunted house.'" Finis, I hope!

AN EPILOGUE

September—1999

I t has been over twenty-five years since we left the House in Hinsdale. In that time, everything has changed. I am writing this addendum from the home in Florence, Oregon, that I share with mum. So much has happened in that time that it's impossible to bring the record up to date. Nevertheless, I will give you a short synopsis.

Phil and I moved to California in April of 1975. After he got a job in San Jose, I returned to New York and picked up Laura and Mary with two of our dogs, Peanuts and Lassie. The three cats, Fluffy, Jinx and Tish were flown out later. In October of 1975, I started working for the City of Santa Clara. However, Phil and I could not sustain our relationship. I finally divorced him in 1980 and, shortly thereafter, resumed my own name. He is now remarried to a woman named Jan and they have a 20 year old daughter named Christine. I remain happily single.

In spring of 1984, I converted to Judaism which seemed to fill the hole left by the ravages of the House and, in 1986, I even made my Bat Mitzvah. *I now call myself a free-spirit and espouse no organized religion.* During the Christmas season in 1984, my mother and I became very ill with what appeared to be severe flu.. The trouble is....my symptoms never fully left me. In February of 1985 mum had a cardiac arrest after I'd taken her to the Emergency Room because she didn't feel well. She had to take it easy for a long time after she came home but recovered fully, which I hear is unusual. My fatigue and muscle aches continued and I was at the doctor for "flu" 18 times in one year. Finally, on my doctor's advice, in December of 1990, I was forced to take a disability retirement from my job as Assistant City Clerk/City Auditor for the City of Santa Clara. It was a few years before my problem was diagnosed as Fibromyalgia and Chronic Fatigue Immune Dysfunction Syndrome. In spite of a wonderful retirement party, I deeply regretted leaving my job. Since living is expensive in California, we moved to Oregon. Now we live on the coast in a lovely immobile, mobile home. It is only a short walk to the ocean and a mile drive to the nearest beach. The scars inflicted by the house, however, have never totally disappeared from our family. In a way, I believe that all our subsequent actions were *influenced* by what happened to us there. *I have never said and do not say now that all our problems were caused by the house. That's a cop-out.*

Incidentally, to answer a question often asked of us: since our family moved out of the house we have been entirely free of "spirit influences". *Hinsdale was our last experience with "ghosts".* So, it wasn't we who were haunted. It was the house.

An update on our family (in 1999): Michael's marriage to a very nice girl named Katie is in the process of being dissolved. The demands of his job as a medical equipment repairman for Lab Performance Specialists were too much for her. He now lives in Carlton, Oregon with their three children: Abraham (17), Peter (15) and Michelle (11). Happily for us, they visit as often as they can.

Beth and Tim live in a lovely home in Lompoc, California. Believe it or not, Tim has retired from the Air Force and is now the Director of Engineering for Spaceport Systems International. It's hard to remember him as the tousle-haired, goofy-hatted young man who patrolled our yards at night now that he's busy sending satellites into orbit. Beth wears many hats. She is the Armed Forces Emergency Services Director for Vandenberg Air Force Base and the District Operations Director of the Santa Barbara County Chapter of the Red Cross. She also teaches International Humanitarian Law and CPR. I don't know what she does in her spare time! She and Tim have two children: Erin (21) who is now in her Senior year at the Air Force Academy and Davey (18) who has just graduated from High School and is attending Junior College preparing for a career in the computer field.

Mary was married in 1989 to a fine young man named George. They now have two sons–George Jr. (9) and Brian (4). They live in a house they recently purchased in Tracy, California. Mary decided, wisely, to take time off from her office manager job to care for the children. George is the Service Manager for Rollins Leasing Corp. in San Jose.

I have left Laura for last. Unfortunately, the prediction of an early death she made in August, 1973 came tragically true. She died on September 1, 1992, just 18 days short of her thirty-second birthday, leaving a husband, Marty, and two sons: Christopher (20) and Jeremy (19), both of whom live with their father and his new wife in San Jose. Marty is retired and the boys are working hard to find themselves. Of all of us, I think Laura was the most affected by the house in the long run. Since we left New York, she had been plagued by bad health and mental problems. It is still undecided whether her overdose on prescription medication was accidental or intentional and it matters little either way. *Laura had always been a firm believer that if one pill helped, two would help more and four would be even better. I was never able to persuade her otherwise.* Now, perhaps, she's at peace. And maybe she even knows what happened in the house.

Of the rest of our cast of characters: my beloved, gentle father died of a pulmonary embolism on June 6, 1979. He had great dreams of coming to live with us in California but never made it. My mother and brother, Gordon, arrived out west in December of 1979.

My brother, Martin, died of cancer on January 3, 1996. His wife Mikki, still lives on Grand Island, New York. Their daughter, Michele, is married and has a daughter, Ashley, and a son, Nicholas. She and her husband, Ron, are in the Air Force and are currently stations at Minot, North Dakota. My sister, Cathie, is divorced and lives with her boyfriend, Dave, and two children, Gary and Karen, in Morgan Hill, California. Gordon, after spending a few happy years with us in Oregon, died from complications of Myotonic (Muscular) Dystrophy on May 17, 1996, just short of five months after Martin.

My girlfriend, Shirl, still lives in Buffalo. Although, a country apart, we still have a very close friendship; in fact I stayed with her when I recently attended the fiftieth reunion of our grammar school graduating class. I have lost track of the other Shirley.

Father Al is still a very close friend. We exchange letters, cards and phone calls frequently. I visited him on my recent trip back east for the above-mentioned reunion. He still receives requests to investigate hauntings and fields questions regarding our house. The Rochester diocese frequently consults him. Despite problems with his health, he hasn't lost one bit of the good-humored vitality that is so much a part of him. A few years ago, he informed me that Alex T, the psychic who had helped us had died (on July 7, 1990). I'm truly sorry because he was a very special man.

Of Michael's friends, I know little. Dave lives near him in northern Oregon. Clarke tried living in California but finally returned to southern New York. Mike N is married and still lives in Hinsdale. Randy also tried California but returned to Hinsdale. The last time I heard about Keith, he was supposedly married to the daughter of an official in Montreal. Debbie and Paul were married and subsequently divorced. Paul called me at work in 1976 but that was the last I heard of him. Beth keeps in touch with some of her friends but I know little of them. As the years pass, circumstances change and people with them.

As for an update on the house: Soon after leaving we learned that the people who had lived in the house twenty-three years before us had asked a priest for help because the house was troubled (I still don't like the word "haunted"). I told a researcher for the Human Dimensions Institute and he checked it out. It was true.

The woman who held our mortgage refused to allow researchers from the above-mentioned Institute, a highly reputable organization affiliated with Rosary Hill College, to go in and see if they could help. Like many people in the area, she apparently thought we had concocted the whole story. *In fact, she accused me of holding "drug parties" at the house!!* I can't imagine anyone being that foolish. If I did make up a story, I assure you, it would certainly make more sense than this one does. The ideal fate for such a house is to become a center for research.

The house has had several families in it since we left. The first, after making much fun of us, moved out and went to Florida within a year.

In the summer of 1978, Ann T, a friend of ours who had a campsite on the corner of the camp road, had a very strange experience. As she sat peacefully reading in the sun, she saw three women pass by. Waving hello, she turned her head back to her book. Suddenly, it dawned on her that she and her husband were the only ones camping in the area. Quickly, she rose and followed the women who disappeared right in front of her eyes as they neared the house. Ann is a practical, down-to-earth person who does not have a vivid imagination. I believe what she saw. When I last spoke with her, she was talking about selling their camp since their two children were grown.

Years after we left the area, I found out that Ann's daughter had a bad experience in their pond. She had been swimming with her twin brother when something grabbed her ankle. The only thing growing on the bottom of the pond was a type of grass so I don't know what it could have been. She swore it was a hand. Her brother had to call her father to pull her out.

Ann also expressed fears for the second tenants to move into our house because they could have been a mirror image of our family. As she watched, the family disintegrated. Soon the wife and children had left and the man was alone in the house. So maybe this story isn't over.

I thought you might be interested in a fascinating tale I heard about the house. Mike was talking to some Navy friends and found out they had lived in Portville at the time of the "haunting". On their leave, they decided to go to the house. They drove up about dusk (remember–the umbrella) and the car quit about half way up the road. They got out and decided to walk. Just as they reached the curve in the road (near the camp road) their car lights turned on and the horn started blaring. They set records getting back to their car and going home.

I remember another incident which I didn't mention in the book. Since I find it amusing, I will relate it here. One day (the date totally escapes me) one of our camping neighbors pulled up in our driveway. I had never met him before but I had noticed that, when he and his family visited their campsite, he was often driving a different car–all of them just one step ahead of junk. This day he was driving a decrepit old Chevy which had seen better days. He was slow spoken and seemed very puzzled.

As far as we knew, he did not know what was going on at our house. He asked if there were something funny about the area in which he camped. Phil asked why and he said because when he had been up at his camp suddenly all his car lights came on. Phil said he probably had electrical problems. Scratching his head, he admitted that was possible but it was still funny since he had no bulbs in any of the lights! He was only puzzled!

Shirl and I visited the house while we were in Olean (in 1999) and it looked sad and neglected. The new owners had painted it brown and the siding and roof were in bad repair. I wouldn't hesitate to go back there to live now that I don't have to worry about the kids. I really loved that house and the type of living it represented.

I would really like to know what happened. I can see, in reading the book, various places that events in the house caused decisions which shaped our future lives. I don't believe our divorce had anything to do with whatever happened there. Phil and I were two entirely different personalities and were bound to split.

There are many things I have omitted either inadvertently or because they made the tale seem even more incredible. I am not at all sure of some of the dates since all my records have disappeared in our many moves but if my friends notice discrepancies, I hope they will forgive me. If there are any errors in the dates they in no way alter the story.

One of the episodes for which I have no date was one of the most enlightening I've ever had. Father Al brought two friends to the house. One, he introduced as a talented psychic with whom he proposed holding a Ouija board session down by the pond. Thank God, he didn't ask us to take part. The other was the man's uncle, a minister. *He was a happy looking man and radiated joy. I liked him immediately. He passed on the Ouija session and said he'd just stroll around. I let him.*

When he came back, he was laughing out loud. He said the house must be a convention center for ghosts....that he'd never seen so many spirits assembled in one place in his life. He proceeded to describe many of those we'd seen and many we hadn't. He said there was a man near the camp road holding a rifle. He was angry at all the trespassers and wanted to keep them off his property. I really wish I knew how to get in touch with him because he impressed me deeply. As for the Ouija board session...nothing happened. I guess the spirits were more interested in the minister.

Of the unbelievable Polaroid snapshot, I have no news. Nor of the film of that strange weekend. The snapshot supposedly disappeared on its return from the Institute for Psychical Research to Alex. In a letter from Alex asking permission to use our name in his book, *Beyond Coincidence*, he said he had put a tracer on the documentary but had heard nothing about it. A letter to Dr. Osis from the Institute for Psychical Research got me no information at all about the picture. When I tried, I could reach no one connected with the movie and was almost tempted to think I imagined it. Alex, too, was baffled by the silence from all parties concerned. At least the mention of that weekend in *Beyond Coincidence* assures me that the film was made.

I hope you have enjoyed my little tale. But I must warn you–I have not made up one thing in this book. It is all true. I, myself, still find it hard to believe but it's all true. I'm always willing to discuss it with anyone hoping they'll come up with a clue I lack. For instance, there was a Regression I went through–but that's another story. I'll leave well enough alone, but I'm always willing to listen.

I wish I had some wisdom to impart as a result of this experience but I don't. I wish I had some insight into the next world but I don't. I can give no answers–only questions. What was in the house? I wish I knew. Is "whatever it was" still there? Time will tell.

When pressed, I will say that I do **not** believe in ghosts. First of all, I think the word is misleading and inaccurate. If a word can carry a lot of baggage, that one does. It conjures up a whole load of preconceptions and puts people immediately on guard. On the other hand, I do believe in **power**. And that's what I believe was at the house. One of the first questions Alex asked me was, "Have you had any UFO sightings in your area?" The query startled me. We had, of course. Did it have anything to do with what followed? Or was it part of the problem? Who knows? I certainly don't.

I have been warned that people will regard this book as fiction. If it pleases them to do so, fine. Or if it makes them feel safer. If you believe our story–congratulations–you have joined a select group. For those in the middle–maybe I've planted a few doubts!

Epilogue to the Epilogue

I don't know if there is really such a thing as an epilogue to an epilogue. If not, I just invented it. I don't know if this news is reassuring or appalling: the house will not die! I should have known that all along. Maybe people need it. There is a deep-seated desire in every human heart to know what comes next. I don't know. It's possible that's why the fascination with so-called ghosts and haunted houses. They assure people about an afterlife without having to espouse any one religion.

Things have changed rapidly since I wrote the epilogue. Mike lives in McMinnville, Oregon with his girlfriend, Linda. His three children live nearby: Abe and Jenny in McMinnville, Peter, Erika and their daughter, Summer, in Yamhill and Michelle and Mike (her Mike) with their son, Logan in Siletz.

Beth and Tim are living in Virginia. Their daughter, Erin moves around with her husband, Charles and sons Connor and Timmy since he's in the Air Force. Davey and his wife, Christal, live in California.

Laura's son, Chris lives in Santa Clara while Jeremy, his wife, Alicia and their daughter, Chelsea, live in San Jose.

Mary and George are moving back to Tracy with their sons, George, Jr. and Brian after an unsuccessful attempt to adapt to the faster, noisier pace of San Jose.

They're all grown up now and life has moved forward. I think, though, the effects of the house in Hinsdale will never completely fade.

Several years ago I received a call from Mike R (the world is full of Mike's). He said he was a medium and I almost hung up. Now I'm glad I didn't. I've never met Mike or his wife, Sheila, yet I consider them close friends. Mike has researched the house and found out many things we were never able to. I've had many calls over the years from people who've read my book but this call was providential. I wish Mike had been around when we needed someone serious to look into what was happening. It's nice to know it's finally happening.

Not too long ago, I also got a call from my old friend, Paul. He was back in Olean and was writing his own book about the house. I welcomed the addition of another testimony and, when I read it, realized it filled in a few holes in my memory and told me things I hadn't known. It's called *You Know They're Here*. The title is in reference to something Laura said to Paul when she realized he knew there were spirits present in the house. As I said, I always called Laura my fey daughter.

Finally, through a series of serendipitous events, I "met" Roger M. Though we met by e-mail and talked on the phone, I consider him a friend as well. He, too, is seriously interested in the house since an early exposure to the place when he was a student at St. Bonaventure University. He, too, filled in some blanks for me. He's now a reporter in Chicago but hopes to assume a teaching post soon.

I watch in amazement and, unfortunately, at a distance, as events once again swirl around the house. Activities there once again raise my hopes that a research foundation will take the place over and find out why the house is so troubled. Is it haunted? Is it in the center of a vortex? Is it affected by the visitation of UFO's? Is it in a "Bermuda Triangle" and doomed by its proximity to ley lines? Is it reflecting the violent events of the past? I just don't know.

At one point when we lived in San Jose, I went to a meeting of a psychic group that met in town. It was headed by a psychic, Sylvia B, who is famous now. When it came time for me to ask a question, I said, "What happened at the house?" That's all I said.

She answered, "You mean as to the fact it was haunted?" I said yes rather sheepishly. I guess she had given me my answer.

Then I said, "What happened to the picture?"

At first she said, "I don't know." but then she corrected herself and said, "It's in a metal box." but she gave no location. So if you have a metal box please check it for a picture of a possible ghost. We were allowed only two questions so I couldn't follow up. For anyone who's interested, I will explain what I meant in the first epilogue when I spoke of straining people's credulity. If you're not interested or I've pushed your trust in me too far, you can stop reading now. When I worked in Santa Clara, a couple of my co-workers asked me to go to a local college for a lecture by a psychic. He was supposed to be able to do group regressions. I was very skeptical but it sounded like fun so I went. We drove to the college in June's very nicely equipped van and were even able to have lunch at the table inside. Eunice was a little apprehensive about the "regression" while I was merely dismissive. June was fascinated. I regret to say, I've forgotten the psychic's name. At any rate, he told us to relax, close our eyes and try to let our minds wander as he named different walks of life. Supposedly, we were supposed to pick up any that had pertained to us in our past lives. Dutifully, I closed my eyes but expected nothing to happen. Wrong again! I should have learned by now not to jump to conclusions.

He mentioned soldier. Suddenly, in my mind, I was somewhere else. Not a soldier but a little boy aboard a ship. I could see what appeared to be tongue-in-groove flooring underneath me, highly polished. I sat behind what must have been a bulkhead and I was terrified. There was fighting going on all around me. I could see blood staining the floor and I knew the ship would sink and I would drown. Is this where my fear of deep water comes from? Though the man was naming different life styles, I seemed to be free-floating. I was a young girl, barefoot, sitting at the foot of a slanting wall. Up high was a small, barred window. The door opened and a man walked in. All I could see was his silhouette. His face was hidden by a cowl. It was the exact same silhouette both Phil and I had seen in our bedroom in Hinsdale one night. The room was dark yet the silhouette was darker than dark. The Inquisition? Again, I knew I was going to die. Then, without warning I was a young girl with long skirts racing across a field toward a house in the distance. Someone was breathing heavily behind me. I assume I was running from him since I was scared to death. I remember slogging across a narrow stream, my feet sliding on the rocks and clambering up the other side. Was this the Hinsdale house? Did I have a relationship with the place a hundred years before? Are we drawn back to places we'd lived in before?

A few years ago I was contacted by another St. Bonaventure graduate. He was now a professor at Texas Christian University and wanted to use my book as a textbook. I was flattered and I hope it helps students to understand things I probably never will. I'd love to take Tim B's class myself but Texas is kind of a long commute.

You see, it's still going on. I get some answers but they only arouse more questions. Maybe I'll never have the answers. Maybe I have to become a ghost myself before I do. If so, I think I'll postpone it for a while. In the meantime ... pleasant dreams, hmm?